DESIGNING A NEWSLETTER

The really, really, really easy **step-by-step guide for absolute beginners of all ages**

Christian Darkin
Series created by Gavin Hoole and Cheryl Smith

LOREM IPSU

Beroyidunto que sum adit, aut autem restibu storrov itinvento tem faquare dolo temquam sequidel sit volenih illorporrum volonis sume quae cus molupta ntumia te corrum fugit, non endi pe uni di berrum rern... que la andae...

Eignat aut o anim et h orum arcu fota pore quae od e... dolorio rporem quae. Mus mod... ero dellab inverferum q aut r... illam et maio custrum recto do... res audae simposandae illia ci test onnim quoditi iscipidi, autemolest tem. Sum ipicia solorrum quam lautet ... ent prepeli gniseide escidelibus es... vento veliquibus, volestiur aut et pos explam dolestrum dolorest, aut aut optatis uta secte.

Dolum qui doluptat et, evendisimus, sapis aut aut qui verum ut dolupisquis ne velitin nihicimi, core ex et ratescium hil ipsam dolupta il eum quaectur max imus dolorep ediscie necerfe... ae la anihilit, qui as ea natiis reptatem harupia nisquis dolorrum idebis erorum, si... exceressinus solupta essumquo dolupta ssecus tem aut quis id quid eossunt...

vollaec... datunt... sum di ductis es... aut aute cum ea... non ni dolo... imus en... tatius sit... quae la si... hillibusa... tatio imus... rum fugia... acestempo... restio entes... quidit eum... qui dolo... doluptat... um... le... quundisQui... aut autem... la unum... v...

Contents

Read this before you start

AVOIDING PITFALLS

Putting together a newsletter, whether it's for a club or society, a political organisation or a company, a special interest group or a local area, can be a daunting prospect. There's a lot to do and a lot to think about, and newcomers to the task often find themselves thrust into the job without much experience in writing, planning or laying out the printed word.In addition, there are plenty of pitfalls – apart from the challenges of creating a great-looking newsletter bursting with fascinating content, there are printing technologies to master, and even legal issues to consider.

That said, the tools available to the newsletter editor today make it quite possible, with a little planning and some grasp of technology, to create publications that look professional and slick. The rise of cheap stock image libraries mean that colourful, professional photos and illustrations are instantly available for a small fee and the page formatting tools provided by the average word processing package make stylish-looking publications quick and easy to put together, once you know how.

THE SKILLS YOU NEED

In this book we'll cover how to organise and run a newsletter. We'll examine the particular styles of writing you need to master to create informative news items and fascinating features. We'll look at the software skills required to lay your publication out on the page, and discover how to make use of a professional printing service to turn it into a professional-looking magazine. Finally, we'll take a look at the options for new media publishing with a few tips on taking your magazine online through websites, email distribution, social networking and even blogging.

 MICROSOFT WINDOWS VISTA HAS BEEN USED FOR THIS BOOK This book assumes that you will have easy access to a computer as well as an internet connection, and the screenshots and procedures given are based on the Microsoft Windows Vista operating system. If you are using a different operating system, you will need to make adaptations accordingly when you work through the step-by-step procedures and refer to the accompanying screenshots.

THE USER-FRIENDLY VISUAL SYSTEM

The same user-friendly visual system as used in all the books in this series makes it really, really, really easy for you to enjoy your first experience of creating a newsletter.

Colour-coded text windows are used so that you can see at a glance the type of information you're looking at:

- introductions and explanations in normal black text on a white background;

- step-by-step action procedures in yellow boxes;

- hints and tips in blue boxes;

- very important notes and warnings in boxes with red borders;

- supportive explanatory information in grey panels.

Where necessary, the detailed procedures are supported by screenshots to make learning easier.

 WORK YOUR WAY THROUGH EACH CHAPTER IN SEQUENCE This step-by-step workbook is designed to be used chapter by chapter. Working through it in its proper sequence will help you do 'first things first' and learn the correct ways of tackling the various processes and methodologies that follow in subsequent chapters.

1 Content

In any newsletter – in any written document – the most important factor is content. It's great to create a good-looking publication, to understand layout and structure and to make your work look good on the page, but those skills are nothing if you can't deliver well-researched, readable articles that are relevant and engaging for your subscribers.

It's not easy to do. It takes thought and planning on your part and there are a few rules to bear in mind, before you start. This chapter should give you a head start, providing tips on how to organise your ideas into a publication that will make sense and how to write the kind of articles your readers, whoever you decide they are, will want to read.

WHAT ARE YOUR AIMS?

Your first job as editor will be to work out exactly what your newsletter is about. This is not as straightforward as it might seem, and for your benefit and the benefit of anyone else involved in the project, it's well worth creating a document which describes in detail exactly what your publication aims to do, how it talks to its readers, who those readers are, and what you do and don't cover and how you set about covering it.

Subject

Defining your subject doesn't just mean deciding to write, for example, a newsletter for your local tennis club. It means knowing in detail just what you will and will not write about. Will you, for example, cover new developments in tennis equipment? Will you print details of tournaments around the world? How will you cover the investigation into irregularities in the club's finances, or the gossip arising from the Christmas party?

These are questions you'll have to answer as events unfold, so having a policy on where you stand before you start will save a lot of problems later on.

Approach

Once you know your subject, you still need to think about your approach to it. The Sun and the Guardian both take news as their subject, but they're very different newspapers.

Write a brief paragraph to remind yourself and contributors to the magazine what tone you're going to take, how formal or relaxed your tone will be and how you will balance entertaining your readers with giving them detailed information.

Readership

Defining your readership is crucial as it will inform both your subject and your approach to it. Who are your readers? What do they like? What are they interested in? Also, just as importantly, how will they approach reading your publication? Will they pick it up and flick through it in a few spare moments, or will they avidly scan it for specific information? Will they have time to sit and read it or will they be snatching a few moments for it in a busy day?

Do they need to be persuaded to pick the magazine up with the use of engaging headlines, puzzles and free offers? Or will they consider reading it cover to cover as a professional or social duty?

Be honest with yourself on these points. The majority of publications that fail do so because they don't correctly understand their readership. The majority of those that succeed do so because readers are committed fans.

Correctly understanding your readership will help make a success of your newsletter

WRITING

Writing for a newsletter or magazine is a particular skill. There are usually firm demands on you as a writer: you have to tell a story. You have to tell it efficiently and accurately and you have to make it interesting. Even the number of words is usually strictly controlled. As you get more used to the process, you'll start to get a feel for structure and the way articles balance and fit together.

Keep your sentences short and to the point. Tell the story, give all the information and then stop. Don't waffle. Don't use flowery language. And never ever go beyond what you know to be true.

Truth and fact

You'll probably be thinking that this last piece of advice doesn't sound like it's followed by many professional news organisations. However, it is. As a test, read a copy of the most biased newspaper you can find. Although you may be infuriated by the assumptions and the omissions in the text, you'll probably find that what facts there are, are actually true (even if they fail to tell the whole story). Newspapers also tend to be very careful in their use of language. For example, if they don't know whether something is true or not, they say 'allegedly' or 'reportedly' in order to cover themselves if what they are saying turns out not to be true.

There's a big gap between fact and truth – and as a journalist, it's up to you to negotiate that.

Impartiality and fairness

Impartiality is another difficult subject in journalism. You can't be truly impartial – just by choosing to cover one story over another, or by asking one question in an interview instead of another you're putting your own skew on the story. Whenever you see a TV report, and the presenter asks the reporter on location to give an assessment of the situation, they're asking for a personal view, not a dry reading of the facts.

Journalists should attempt
to be fair, if not impartial

A good journalist isn't there to be impartial. He's there to be the reader – to ask the questions the reader would have asked and to represent their concerns while at the same time giving the reader the information they need to inform those concerns.

So whilst it's not really about impartiality, it is about fairness – about putting the points which don't support the views you hold as strongly as those that do. It's about being as tough on your friends as your enemies and trusting that if you're really right about your own opinions, the readers will come to those conclusions just by being given the facts you have.

The more important the story, the more people reading it will have their own opinions and the more critical they will be of the way you cover it. You will be accused of bias whether you're fair or not, and the only way to defend yourself against those accusations will be to have the facts laid out in the article.

Writing the lead story

If you're writing one of the main news items for your magazine, you might have anything from 500 to 2000 words to play with, but there are some important rules to follow. The first, and the one most usually and infuriatingly ignored by novice journalists, is the 'Top Line' or 'Standfirst'.

The Top Line is the first couple of sentences of the article. Some publications print the top line in bold just to highlight it. The idea is that if your reader reads only the first sentence, they must come away with the essence of your article. No ifs, no buts. The Top Line tells the story.

The paragraphs that follow the Top Line may elaborate, add quotes from important players in the story, bring in the arguments or viewpoints of opposing sides, or give more information. However, your reader will quickly give up if they're not clear by the first couple of lines exactly what has happened and why they should be interested in it.

Try to use other people's perspective rather than your own to tell the story. Having you describe a fire somebody's told you about is much less interesting than hearing their account of their escape from it. Hearing you explain why a prize was awarded is just conjecture – quoting directly from the judge is more immediate and informative.

The Top Line of an article gives the essence
of the story and will draw in the readers

Likewise, don't just say something is controversial – say who's criticising it and on what grounds.

Use active, concise and dramatic language. Don't say 'there was a significant upward trend in year-on-year membership figures in numerical terms'. Say 'membership is up' or, if you want to stress it 'membership went through the roof'.

 IMPORTANT **If you quote people, quote accurately. If you claim somebody has said something, you'd better be sure they have said it because if they haven't they can sue you for defamation.**

Finally, the last paragraph of a news piece should sum up the story. That's not the same as the first paragraph's introduction to the story – it's a summing up of what the reader has learnt by reading the intervening story.

Short news items

Short news items – usually between 50 and 250 words – are used for less crucial, but still noteworthy and interesting pieces of information. Again, the Top Line is vital. Get it right and the rest will follow.

You'll constantly find there isn't enough space to tell the full story in a short news item, but treat that as a challenge, not a restriction. The size limitation isn't just made up – it's based on what people are prepared to read, and are able to digest in a short time. In other words, keeping your writing brief and to the point isn't just about saving paper, it's about getting a story across that simply would not be read if it was any longer.

Clarity is fundamental, so it's important to understand your reader – after all, you need to know what background information you can safely cut out because they already know it allowing you to jump straight to the important events.

With really short news items (50 words or so), all you've got time to do is let the audience know the bare facts, so remember the fundamentals: who, what, where, when and why. Cover these in two sentences without misrepresenting anyone or oversimplifying and you're on your way to being a good journalist.

Leave the reader wanting to know more – and give them some way to find out more (a web link, or a clue in the text about sources of further information is good).

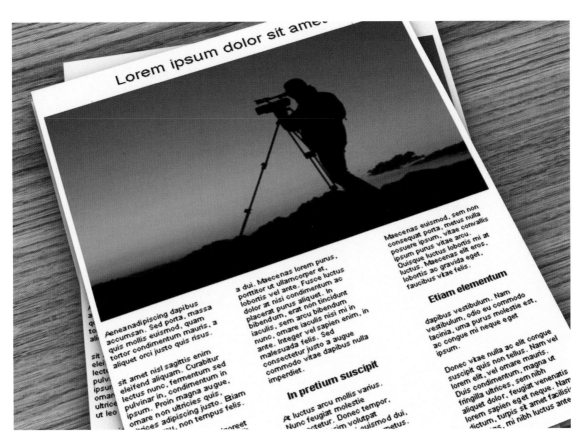

Feature articles are in-depth and often entertaining

Features

Features are something different again. Buried in the centre of your publication, feature articles are longer than news stories and more in-depth. They're also less dependent on hard facts and instead concentrate on colour – giving the reader a feel for a subject. This is no excuse for over-writing. Word counts are still strictly controlled (800–2000 words is usual).

Writing a good feature is, if anything, even harder than writing a news item. Once you know the story, and your angle on it, a news story usually writes itself. A feature requires you to uncover the story and tell it in an entertaining way that will keep the reader interested even without the impact of a hard news headline. This puts your writing style centre-stage.

TIPS: FEATURE WRITING

The only way to get a real feel for feature writing is to read lots, and write lots. However, here are a few helpful tips:

FIND AN ANGLE It's not enough to report a lot of interesting information in a list. You need to find an angle on it – preferably a human angle. The details of how a steam engine was renovated isn't interesting in and of itself. The problems encountered by someone struggling to do it is.

TELL A STORY Look for the drama and the way things change rather than relaying a series of static positions. Stories have a beginning, a middle and an end, and you need to find these in the story you write. This advice can sound as though you're being asked to invent a story – but you're not. The story is there in every article you write because otherwise you wouldn't want to write it. Your job is to strip away the distracting elements and present it in its purest form.

COLOUR Adding colour to a piece means bringing in details, which fill out and expand on the story. These are the things which interest and entertain the reader and make them care about the story you're telling. They're not the main story itself, but they do compliment it and bring it into focus.

STYLE Don't go over the top in trying to discover your own writing style and impress it on your work. It'll just look forced. Instead, let it develop, concentrate on your subjects and your own voice will come through naturally.

Headlines and sub-headings

Headlines and subheadings instantly help to set the style of your publication. You know a tabloid headline from a broadsheet one as soon as you see it, and you can tell a Cosmo article title from one printed in the Economist – not just because of the subject matter, but because of the tone.

You should know before you write a line what kind of publication you're creating, and headlines and sub-headings will reflect this. That said, whatever your newsletter's style, headlines have the same, important jobs. Here's a checklist:

Does your headline:
- Tell the truth?
- Show the article's viewpoint on the story?:
- Tell the reader what to expect from the article?
- Tell the reader what to expect from the publication?
- Provoke an emotional reaction?
- Make the reader want to read the article?
- Get all these messages across in as small a number of words as possible?

Hold the back page

The back page of a periodical is often treated as just a bit of fun, but it's got a vital job to perform. It's there to give your readers another reason to pick up your publication – a reason that has nothing, or very little to do with the publication's main job, but which develops a rapport between you and your readers on a whole other level.

The back page is about getting your readers involved. It's about being interactive with them, and it's about giving them a bit of light relief.

Here are a few suggestions for the back page of your newsletter:

Puzzles and Quizzes – How many people do you know who claim to buy the newspaper they do just for the crossword? Adding a suduku, a crossword or a quiz will give readers a reason to pick up the magazine, and while they're there, they might just read some of your more important features.

Choose interactive content for your back page

Coming soon – you probably know just as many people who insist they buy a magazine just for the TV guide. If you can provide information on upcoming events – whether that's local cinema or theatre news, concerts, TV or even just sales, people will have a reason to keep reading.

Competitions – Get a local firm to offer prizes and you've not only got a reason for readers to pick up the magazine, you've also got a reason for them to write or email in.

Letters – offer readers a forum in the publication to discuss events, or even criticise your coverage. The result will be a readership who feels valued and who has a stake in the newsletter itself.

Cartoons – Cartoons offer a bit of light relief and they're a relief from the blocks of text offered by the rest of the magazine. If they've got a continuing theme from issue to issue, then so much the better.

PICTURES AND COPYRIGHT

Every good newsletter deserves pictures. Big blocks of dense text are a turn-off to even the most interested reader, and even if you are going for the kind of magazine that prints 3,000 word features, you'll improve your magazine no end if you break them up with a few relevant images.

Even the famous scientific journal, *Nature* – whose primary purpose is to publish scientific research papers – employs artists to spice up their publication with well chosen illustrations.

Think about how your magazine will look right at the beginning of production. Get used to thinking about how every article and story will be illustrated at the same time as you think about how it will be written. This will help the pictures and the article hang together as a sensible package.

If someone else is writing the story, find out if they can provide photos and illustrations. If it's you, make a note during your research and interviews of any images that might be useful.

Well-chosen pictures help to break up blocks of text

Illustration

Sometimes, an illustration will work better than a photo. Illustrations generally fall into two categories – diagrams designed to illustrate a specific theme in the text, and artworks whose purpose is to entertain as much as to inform.

The first category can be anything from simple charts or line drawings through to highly creative and detailed images. The key here is to get the information across, so clarity is everything.

The second category gives you a chance to have a bit of fun with the subject, giving it a different angle or providing a new take on something in the text. These sort of illustrations are usually printed large at the beginning or in the middle of the text.

TIP: PHOTOGRAPHS

There are plenty of books on how to take good photographs, and we won't try to replace them here. However, there are a few tips to remember when taking photographs for newsletters:

ACTION Try to photograph things happening rather than photographing just things. A picture of a dancer dancing is far more interesting than a photo of them posing in an office.

PEOPLE Get photographs of the main people involved in a story, but try to do it in a context that reflects the story. A photo of a fireman out of uniform is just a photo of a man.

PERMISSION Make sure you have written permission to photograph whoever and wherever you need to if you can. That way, you won't loose that all important shot while you try to negotiate whether you're allowed to be there.

EVENTS You rarely know about a news event before it happens, but in the case of an organised event, you do – and that means you can be there in place to get the perfect picture. Don't waste that opportunity.

SAY SOMETHING A picture can be worth a thousand words. However, it can be worth none. Look for photo opportunities that say something you can't say in the article. The look on someone's face when they win an award – the mud on the side of a rally car after a race – the scale of a new exhibit in a museum.

Look for pictures that are engaging and tell the story

Commissioning

Having photographers (and illustrators) on hand for your magazine is always a great help. Just the fact that someone else is thinking about how the magazine will look, and what images need to be located will be a massive weight off your mind.

Make sure you give whoever is taking your photos clear instructions about what you want. Make sure they know as much as possible about what your story is going to be and what angle you're approaching it from, and if there's any kind of event to be covered try to make sure they're there in good time to capture the main action. After that, let the photographer get on with it themselves. Don't be tempted to constantly tell them what to do and where to stand.

If photos of the main event aren't possible, portraits of the main characters involved, or important objects will have to do, but a photo of something happening is always more interesting.

TIP: COPYRIGHT

Photos and illustrations are copyrighted automatically. If someone takes a photo or draws a sketch and you publish it – in any form – without permission, you can be sued.

Just to make life harder, you can also be sued by anyone pictured in any of your photos, or the owners of any property or trademarks you show unless you have their permission.

However, if you're using the photo in an editorial context – that means as part of a news item or information piece, and you're not trying to sell anything, or infer anything untrue about the person or property featured – you are allowed to use the picture.

In other words, you can print a photo of someone's 100th birthday party in a news item, but you can't use the picture as an advert for your range of birthday cakes without permission from everyone in the photo. Additionally, if it turns out that the guest of honour was actually only 97, they can sue.

Furthermore, if you didn't get permission from whoever took the picture, you can't print it no matter what it shows or how you want to use it. The only exception to this is if the photographer has been dead for more than 50 years.

Don't ignore this. It happens all the time. Get permission for any photo you're not sure about, and get it in writing. Have a brief document or email you can get people to sign and return to you and you won't have anything to worry about.

High-quality stock images have helped improve the look of amateur publications

Stock libraries

You may have noticed over the last few years that newsletters in general have got – well – a lot better looking. One of the main reasons for this is the cheap and easy availability of high-quality stock imagery.

Stock photos and illustrations used to be the preserve of high-budget magazines who saw paying £100 or more per photo as a cheap way to get high quality generic images.

The rise of the Internet, however, created a demand for much cheaper, much more freely available pictures, and the so-called micro-stock sites appeared to fill that gap.

Nowadays, although specialist images are still sold by traditional stock libraries and still attract significant prices, there are millions of very high quality, very professional photos and illustrations which you can buy for a couple of dollars and use for whatever purpose you like. Photographers will get paid just a tiny amount each time you buy one of their photos, but because a popular image can sell hundreds or even thousands of times, it can be well worthwhile for them.

Because stock image libraries understand the importance of copyright issues, there are strict guidelines for photographers. Any photo you buy will be free of copyright restrictions and will have all the required permissions already granted.

A stock library is a great place to search if you're looking for a photo of a famous landmark, a generic shot of a factory, or an illustration depicting a certain activity or emotion. You'll struggle, if you're looking for very specific or specialist images.

TIP: STOCK IMAGE SITES

www.istockphoto.com
www.shutterstock.com
www.dreamstime.com

PREPARING THE GROUND

By now, you should have a fair idea of what your newsletter will contain. You should know about its style and content, and how it's going to communicate this information to the readers.

However, right now, it's just an idea in your own mind. What you need to do next is start to organise your publication, and the people who will be helping you put it together. You need a set of formal documents that will guide everyone involved through exactly what they need to do for each issue, and a set of deadlines to ensure that the magazine goes to press on time and in good order.

The next chapter will provide you with the tools you need to create the organisational structure which will help your publication run smoothly from issue to issue.

2 Organisation

Putting together a newsletter is a big job. There is a lot of skill involved, and even if most of the work is going to be done by one person, you'll need to carefully plan to make sure everything is done on time and to a high standard. This chapter should give you a few ideas about how to organise the work, how to break the production down into jobs, and how to set deadlines that will make sure your magazine always comes out on time.

PUBLICATION DATE

Your first decision has to be how often you are going to publish the magazine. A yearly publication will of course have a completely different set up from a weekly newsletter.

Periodicals

A yearly or quarterly journal will most likely be a big publication with plenty of room for long thoughtful articles. It's not likely to contain a lot of news or gossip, and readers are likely to keep it for longer, so, it lends itself to documentation, and reference material. The long lead time means that can be (and needs to be) meticulously researched and carefully worded. It also means that publication deadlines will be a big deal. If you get something wrong, you won't have a chance to correct it until the next issue.

Style is dictated by the frequency of publication

In addition, contributors, editors and anyone else working on publication will never have the chance to get into the swing of things and establish patterns of working. This means you have to be very clear in setting up the style and layout of the magazine in a way that everyone involved can pick up and understand very quickly.

Weekly and monthly publications

Newsletters that are produced more often tend to be smaller. They tend to be more quickly disposed of, more responsive to news and events, less formal, and more interactive with their readers.

Shorter deadlines mean the editor needs to be working on the next issue before the previous one is published, and needs to be stricter about deadlines and schedules. Having articles held in reserve, in case a feature you're expecting doesn't materialise, is essential. As is getting a rhythm going amongst everyone involved in the publication so that you can rely on everybody to deliver what they've promised in good time, and in a format you're expecting.

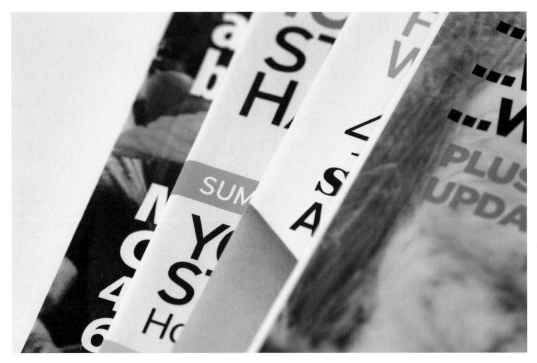

Your publication will need a different schedule depending on whether it is weekly or monthly

A regular publication requires discipline and teamwork. You have to develop good working relationships, and everybody will have to recognize that the publication is a commitment.

Regular magazines change and evolve over time, as the needs of their contributors and their readers change, and as an editor it's essential for you to listen to both constantly.

SET UP A PRODUCTION SCHEDULE

Whether you're working yearly, weekly, monthly or quarterly, you'll need to break each issue down into deadlines. If you have a list of dates on which certain aspects of the magazine have to be completed, then everyone will always know where they stand and what has to be done. If you don't, and simply let people know when you're due to publish, you'll risk not getting key articles or artwork ready in time, and the whole magazine will have to be thrown together at the last moment.

To create a list of deadlines, work backwards from your publication date. Here's an example deadline list of deadlines for a monthly magazine:

EXAMPLE OF A PRODUCTION SCHEDULE

1st April	Publication date All copies have to be distributed today, so you need to organise delivery, or postage. This often involves a team of dedicated drivers or envelope stuffers.
25th March	The magazine has to be printed and checked by today.
15th March	All desktop publishing work must be finished, and the files containing the finished magazine must be sent to the printers in time for any problems to be resolved.
10th March	News deadline This is the final deadline for any news items and any changes to the text of the magazine. Anything that comes in after this date has to wait for next issue. At this stage, the editor needs to have written any editorials, letters pages, or other last minute content.
5th March	Layout During this week, the articles, artwork and photos have to be edited and arranged on the page. Anything you don't have by now, isn't going in.
1st March	Advertising deadline Advertising for this issue has to have been submitted by today. All the artwork for the adverts should have been provided ready to print. If you're laying the adverts out yourself, you'll need to make this deadline earlier to give yourself a chance to do this.
1st March	Copy deadline All articles, photos and artwork need to have arrived with you ready to be put into the magazine. This gives you time to read through them, ask for any re-writes and if necessary, replace articles that aren't working. Most editors will stagger their copy deadlines for different articles throughout the month so that they have plenty of time to work through any problems.
20th February	Final commissioning deadline Everything that's going into the magazine needs to have been commissioned by now. The editor will know by this date exactly what's going into the magazine and how many pages it will fill. The editor will also be forming an idea of how the publication will be arranged and how the articles will balance each other. The contributors will know what they have to produce, how many words their articles will be, how they will be arranged (whether the article is one block of text or whether there are separate sections) and what they will cover. Any photography or illustration will have also been commissioned.
February	Writing and research anyone submitting articles for the magazine will need to be in the process of researching and writing them this week. Any problems with this need to be reported to the editor immediately to give them time to re-assess.
February	Advertising the process of finding advertisers for the magazine (if it has any) can't begin early enough. It's a difficult process and will go alongside the publication process. As soon as the editor knows what's going to be in this issue, adverts that compliment those articles can be sought.
1st February	First commissioning deadline Anything that doesn't involve up-to-date news (i.e. fiction, quizzes, 'feature' style articles and longer, discussion pieces) will have been commissioned by today. The contributors will know what they have to produce and when.
January	The editor is thinking through what's going to appear in April's issue, deciding on the main features, and the main thrust of the issue. This is the time he or she has to come up with the big ideas, which will shape the issue and it's worth talking to contributors now about any ideas they have.

TIP: PLANNING AHEAD

As you can see, even with tight deadlines for everything, the monthly magazine you receive at the beginning of April will have been conceived in January. Last-minute news is still possible right up to the middle of March, but the editor should know pretty much what the contents page will say by mid February. In other words, concentrate on being thorough rather than up-to-date.

Roles will need to be assigned

PEOPLE

Most professional monthly magazines are run by a dedicated staff of 4–5 people – as well as lots of freelance writers, photographers, illustrators and contributors who each provide one or two pieces of work for each issue.

If you have other people willing to work on your project, here are a few jobs you can allocate to make the process run smoothly:

Publisher The cash behind the magazine. The publisher puts up the money and appoints the editor (and therefore everyone else). The publisher can be directly involved in the magazine, but usually restricts themselves to deciding where in the marketplace it's positioned, and how the publication develops over time.

Editor Ultimately responsible for the content of the publication. The editor decides what goes in, and how it's arranged. If the magazine represents anyone's view of the world, it's the editor's. If the magazine is a particularly large one, there may be several assistant editors. There may be a news editor, a features editor, a sports editor, etc. All of these will report to the overall editor.

Sub editor Responsible for taking each article, checking it and editing it so that it fits in with the overall style of the magazine, and so that the words fit correctly on the page – filling the required columns. The Sub editor ensures consistency in the tone and language of the magazine, and if there are spelling and grammatical errors, or if facts are incorrect, it's down to them.

Picture editor Sources, commissions, and gets permission for any photography or illustration in the magazine and decides (with help from the editor), which pictures go where and what publication's front cover looks like. The picture editor may spend their time searching for photos online, securing permission to use other people's images, collecting historical images or commissioning new photography or illustration.

The editor has ultimate responsibility

Layout artist Arranges images and words on the page. Decides on fonts, styles, and handles the look of the entire magazine. The layout artist decides how the columns are laid out, where the pictures fit on the page, how big the headlines are. The layout artist is the reason that Heat magazine looks different from Vogue.

Writers Most of the writing for most magazines is done by freelancers employed to write specific articles. This allows the magazine to choose the best person for each assignment and allows the writer to specialise and get to know his subject well. Some magazines also have staff writers, producing the more general content.

Photographers The photographer's roll depends on the kind of magazine you're publishing. Some magazines send out a photographer with every journalist and have features where the pictures are more important than the words (i.e. fashion magazines). Others use pictures simply to illustrate what's going on in the text. Either way, the photographer needs to know what the Picture Editor needs, and be acutely aware of how their images will be used.

Freelance staff is often employed

Advertising sellers Responsible for selling advertising space in the magazine, approaching sponsors and bringing in the cash. Usually there will be a set of rates for different sizes and types of advertising (within which negotiations take place) and the publication should have strict policies about what advertising it takes, how it places it and what it is and is not prepared to sell.

TIP: THE PLACE OF ADVERTISING

The relationship between advertising (if there is any) and editorial content varies hugely from one magazine to another. Most publications value their independence highly, and the best way to ensure this independence is to have the advertising side run by a separate person from the editorial side. An editor who is also responsible for finding adverts will find it much harder to keep the articles he publishes independent.

That said, a strong relationship between advertisers and editors can also be helpful as long as their aims are similar – with advertisers providing access to information and help the magazine wouldn't otherwise get.

The key is to make sure that any advertising is driven by the content of the magazine, not the other way around. For example, an advert for the films being shown at a local cinema might sit very well alongside a review of those films, but the cinema has to understand that if your reviewer doesn't like the films, he will say so.

FORMATTING DOCUMENTS

When setting up the magazine, it's a good idea to have a set of documents that you can give to anyone involved in the publication to let them know exactly how your magazine is supposed to look and feel.

House style

House style covers things like the tone writers should adopt, the length of articles, the level of detail and complexity, how formal or conversational, the writing is supposed to be, and what level of knowledge writers should assume the readers have.

However, it also covers the fine detail that makes the magazine consistent. For example: Are numbers written numerically (400) or in words (four hundred)? Do you use abbreviations? Do you say 'are not' or aren't? Do you follow a full stop with one space, or two?

These things might seem unimportant, but keeping them consistent helps to give your magazine a unified and polished feel.

Article format sheet

An article format sheet tells the writer exactly what he or she needs to provide for each piece of writing. A typical article format sheet is like a form for the writer to fill in. Here's an example for an 'events' section:

- **Headline** (maximum five words):
- **Subtitle** (15 words):
- **Main body of article** (75 words describing the event):
- **Information box** (address and contact details):

Each type of article in your magazine will have its own format sheet. You might have one format for your main news item, another format for your smaller news items, and a third format for a longer feature article. Once you have format sheets, for all the different types of articles you publish, it'll become a lot easier to commission articles, and to fit them into your magazine once they're written.

There's nothing to stop you adapting and changing your format sheets as you go along, or even breaking the rules in them for particular articles. But creating them means that you've always got a template into which you can fit your magazine without having to re-work everything from scratch for each issue.

TIME TO START WORK

By now, you should have decided on the basic form of your newsletter, how often it's going to be published and what's going to be in it. Your diary will be full of dates and deadlines leading up to publication, and you'll have written documents describing what each type of article will contain and how it will be presented.

It's now time to look at how the whole thing comes together on the page as we learn the tools of desktop publishing.

3 Formatting

This chapter deals with the technical side of laying out your newsletter for publication using a word processing package. If you're comfortable with your software, or if you have your own choice desktop publishing package you plan to make use of, you can skip this section. However, whatever your skill level, it's worth taking a quick look at the tutorials in this chapter as the techniques can be adapted to whichever package you're using and will stand you in good stead when you come to put your newsletter together on paper.

The creative choices and artistic side of producing your newsletter's look and feel are dealt with in the next chapter. Here, we're only concerned with how to get from the bare text of an article and a few photos to a neatly laid out and readable magazine.

SOFTWARE: MICROSOFT WORD

We're going to concentrate on using Microsoft Word – not because it's particularly the best package on the market for the newsletter publisher, but simply because it's the most popular. A version of Word (or its slightly cut-down version, Microsoft Works) is likely to already be installed on your PC or Mac.

TIP: OPEN OFFICE

If you don't have Word, then try an alternative; Open Office (visit www.openoffice.org for more information). Open Office is a completely free package, but it's a good one, and it's been written to mimic Word in almost every way. There are occasional differences in features, and sometimes you'll find menu items or tools hidden in different places, but basically, you'll be able to follow everything in this chapter regardless of whether you're working with Word or Open Office.

 Your version of Word might look different from the one in our images depending on when and where you bought it. Everything in this chapter can be done on all current versions and any copy going back to 2003.

SOFTWARE: OTHER OPTIONS

There are, of course, other word processors on the market (most of them containing largely the same tools and features). There are also more specialist Desktop Publishing (DTP) packages available at all levels. These contain tools to make laying out documents very easy, and flexible. Here are a few:

Adobe InDesign and Quark Xpress

Both top of the range packages, producing professional results with prices to match. Almost every magazine you pick up in a shop will have been produced using one of these professional packages. You can get similar results with much cheaper software though if you're prepared to put in the effort.

A sample page in Adobe InDesign

Microsoft Office Publisher

This package features many of the same tools and layouts as Word, but with an emphasis on page layout. Publisher may or may not be included in your version of Microsoft Office, but unfortunately you can't buy it without buying the rest of Office. If you do have it, you can transfer a lot of the advice here to working with Publisher.

Serif PagePlus

This is one of the best offerings at the cheaper end of the market. Page Plus is popular among small organisations, clubs and societies. It's easy to use and there's even a free version available to get you used to the toolset. If you're going to buy a dedicated DTP package, you could do a lot worse than this one.

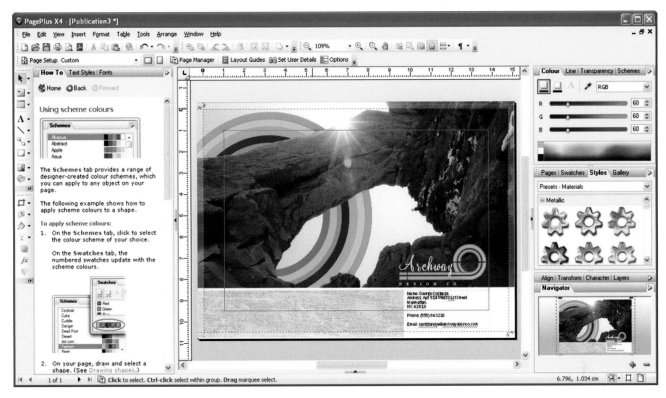

How your screen may look if you are using Serif PagePlus

INTRODUCTION TO WORD

As software goes, Microsoft Word is about the most common package around. At it's simplest level, it's also one of the easiest to pick up. Just open it and start typing. Click Save on the File menu at the top to save. Click Open on the same menu to load a new document.

That, even for people who use the package very day – even for most professional writers and journalists – is pretty much as far as they go with the package. All the other buttons, icons and menu items get ignored. This is a pity, because in reality, Word is far more than just a typewriter. With it, you can lay out text on the page, alter its look and size, create headlines, bullet points and columns, and add photos and illustrations. You can save your finished files as Internet pages, text documents or (with a little addition that we'll come to in chapter 5), as PDF documents ready to send to a professional printing company.

Basic Word

This tutorial gives a basic grounding in Word. It'll let you know in a few short steps how to change fonts, create headlines, check and align your text. Start here if you're unsure about your way around the package. If you're more confident, feel free to skip this section.

1 If you've got Word on your system, you'll find it on the Start Menu. Usually, it'll be listed fairly near the top. If not, try clicking **All programs** at the bottom of the start menu, and looking for a folder labelled **Microsoft Office** or something similar.

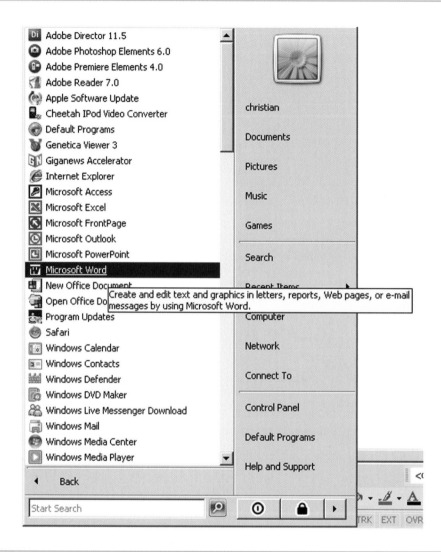

2 Add some text. Type in a few paragraphs, then click **Save** on the File menu to save your work. You can select blocks of text, single words or letters by holding down the left mouse button and dragging. The text will turn from black on a white background to white on a black background. Any commands you apply will apply only to selected text.

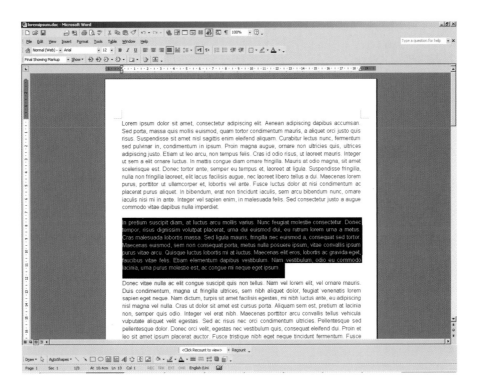

3 You can now move the text around by releasing the mouse button, then clicking again and dragging to place the text somewhere else. You can also use **Cut** or **Copy** from the Edit menu, and then move the cursor to a different point in your document (or another document entirely) and select **Paste** from the Edit menu to paste the text back in. (You can use Ctrl X and Ctrl V).

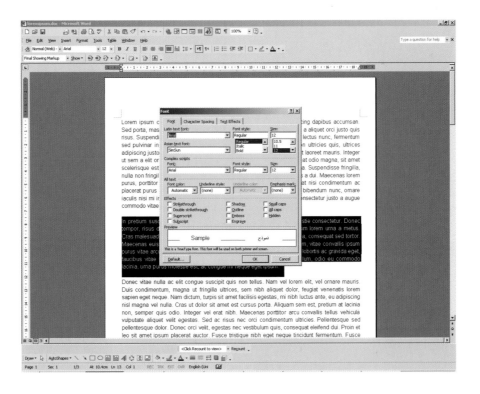

4 Try selecting a few words and clicking the **B**, **I** or **U** icons on the top toolbar. Your text is now made bold, italic or underlined (click the icon again to remove the effect). You can also use the dropdown list to the left of or above the 'B' icon to change the size of the text, or the list to the left of that to change the typeface (font).

TIP: FONT FEATURES

If you want more control over your text, right click and choose Font from the menu, and you'll be able to adjust many more features of your text and add other effects like shadows, outlines, colours, underlining, embossing and engraving.

---

5 Take a look at the four icons to the right of the 'U' icon. These control the way text is positioned on the page. The left hand one lines any selected text up to the left hand margin. The next one centres your text, the one after that lines it up to the right hand margin. The final icon 'justifies' your text (stretches each line so it lines up with the left and the right margins creating a solid block of text).

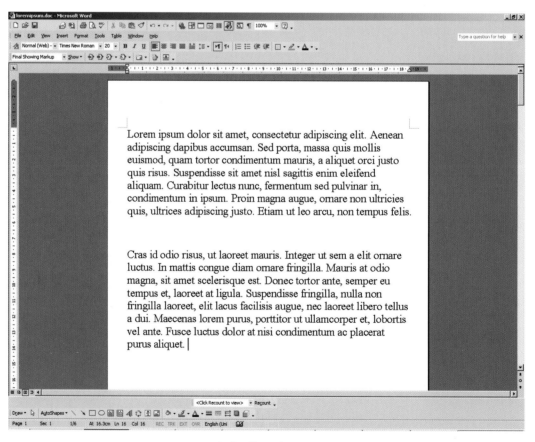

Left-aligned text

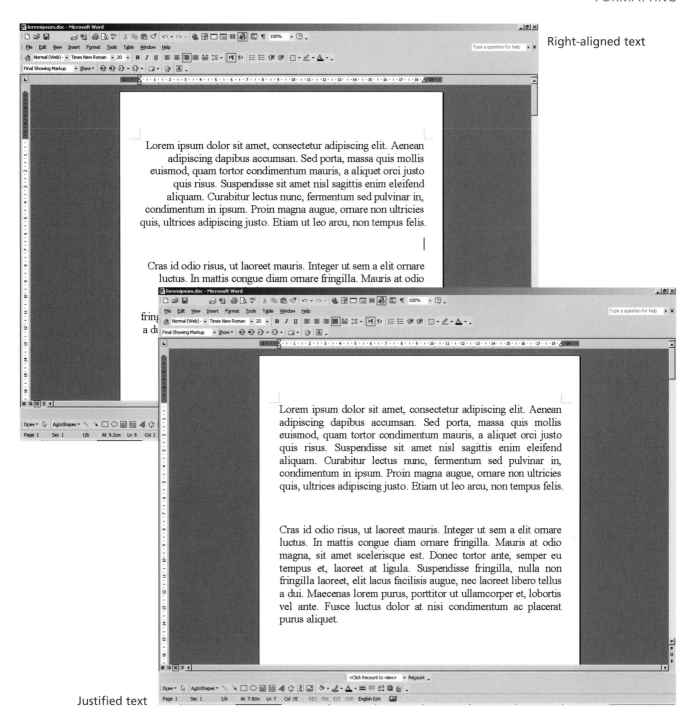

Right-aligned text

Justified text

6   When Word underlines your text in red, it's letting you know it thinks you've made a spelling mistake (right click on the word to correct it). When it underlines in green it thinks you've made a grammatical error and right clicking will offer solutions. Word's interpretation of grammar is quite strict, and often suggests corrections when you're simply using casual modern language. You can safely ignore either red or green markings if you think they're wrong. Neither will ever appear in your printed document. To run a spell check, go to the Tools drop down menu and select **Spelling and Grammar.**

7 Word also provides a few automatic tools, which can be helpful (or irritating depending on your situation):

- If you put in a row of '-' signs (hyphens), then hit Return, Word will automatically turn it into a neat, solid line right across the page or column. This is useful for breaking up blocks of text.
- If you start a paragraph with a number and hit Return, Word creates a new paragraph labelled with the next consecutive number. If you go in and add more paragraphs in the middle, Word will automatically re-number for you.
- The same happens if you start a paragraph with 'a)' or 'a.'. If you want to alter the formatting of this numbering system (or remove it completely) just double click on one of the numbers or letters and a dialogue will appear allowing you to replace the numbers with dots, alter the layout or remove them completely.

8 If you choose **Word Count** from the Tools menu, Word will let you know how many words, paragraphs, pages, characters and lines are in your document. If you select a block of text, you can also see how many words you've selected. This is an essential tool for anyone involved in newsletters. Everything in professional writing comes down, in the end, to word counts. Every block of text on every page needs to be of a tightly controlled length or your whole publication will quickly get out of hand. This paragraph, for example, is nearing 100 words, so it's time to end it.

9 In order to print your document, simply use the **Print** option from the File menu. Assuming you have a printer plugged in, switched on and correctly installed, your document will be printed.

Toolbars

Word is adaptable and customisable. The tool bar at the top of the screen has a range of buttons that you probably don't use much. The good news is you don't have to have them there. Right click on an empty part of the toolbar and you can add or remove toolbars depending on your use of the package. If you're not going to be using word art (which is largely rubbish) you can turn that toolbar off. If you want to have a word count constantly displayed, turn on the 'word count' tool.

1 At the bottom of the toolbar list is a **Customise** option. Select this, and choose the commands tab and you can see a list of icons for virtually every command and menu item available in Word. Drag any of these to the toolbar and they'll stick, so any command you use regularly will appear as a handy button whenever you run Word.

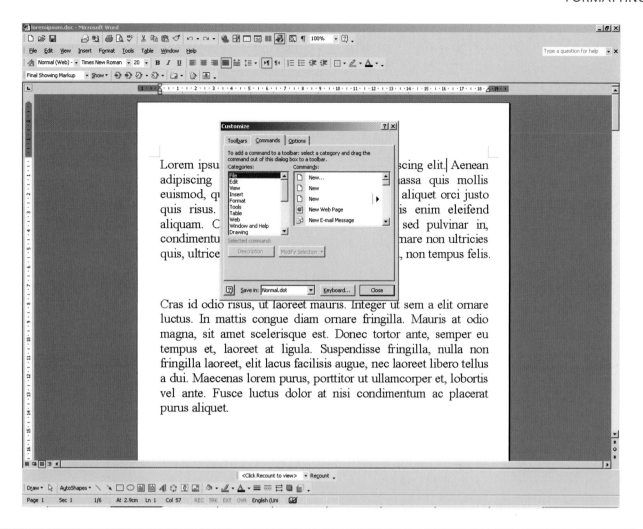

TIP: VANISHING MENU ITEMS

As you use Word, it adapts to you, so if you don't use items on the menus for long periods of time, they will disappear so that when you open the menu you won't have to spend ages looking through options you never use. If you're expecting to find a menu item and it's vanished, click the double downward arrow at the bottom of the menu list and all your old menu items will reappear.

TWO WAYS TO LAY OUT YOUR MAGAZINE

As far as magazine layout goes, there are basically two different ways to work: the easiest way and the most flexible way. Each has its advantages, and you can mix and match methods if you want to, but the method you choose will depend on your level of skill with the package and the complexity of your newsletter.

The easy way

The simplest way to use Word to layout your newsletter is to take a piece of writing and format it directly on the page. Here's a quick guide:

1 Bring in an article by either loading up, pasting in, or typing a document. Make it a couple of pages in length and make sure it's got a headline and a couple of sub-headings somewhere in the middle. This will give you something to work with.

2 Create a headline. Start by selecting the title (click and drag over it) and choose **Font** from the format menu (you can also bring up this dialogue by right clicking on the selected text). Change the size from 12 to 22 or more and the font style to Bold. If you like, you can also change the Font itself – Arial Black is always a good headline font.

3 To centre and space, use the **Centre** button or right click and select **Paragraph**. Change **Alignment** to **Centred**, then hit **Return** to create some space between the headline and the main text.

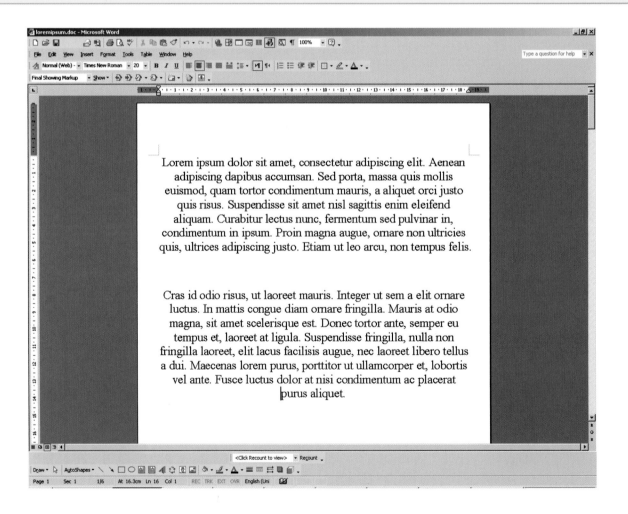

4 To create columns, select the main body of your text and from the Format menu, choose Columns. A column dialogue appears allowing you to format the selected text into as many columns as you like. You can choose the number of columns, control the spaces between them, define whether they're of equal sizes and decide whether to put a dividing line between columns. Choose 3 columns of equal size without a line between them, and a 0.5cm spacing.

5 To format the text with the main body text still selected, use the same methods outlined above to reduce the font size from 12 point to 9 point. Your page should now be looking a lot more like a newsletter.

6 Make the subheadings bold, and slightly larger than the surrounding text. Put them in the same font as the main headline, and centre them. Choose the first paragraph of the story and make it bold, then locate the end of the first story and finish it off with a row of '-' signs (hyphens). Hit **Return** and this should change into a solid line.

Extra stories

You've now got the start of the layout for a newsletter, but there are a couple of problems. The first is that right now you have one headline for the whole newsletter. No problem – let's make one of our sub-headings into a main headline for a new story. Select the headline, change its size to match the top headline and select **Columns** from the Format menu. Now choose **1 single column**, and your columns will divide. Your headlines at the top and in the middle will stretch right across the page, and above and below, the main text will remain in columns.

The second problem is that as you change the text, the length of the newsletter changes. Let's say you've got one story on the front page, two on the next page and a back page with some other information. If you now change a single word on page 1, your whole format will shift and you'll have to re-adjust it. The answer is to decide where you want each page to end, place your cursor there, and choose **Break** from the Insert menu. You can then select **Page Break** or **Column Break**, and no matter how you alter the text on the preceding page, your new page (or column) will always start at the same point in the text.

TIP: SHOWING HIDDEN PAGE BREAKS

If you've put in page breaks, but you've forgotten where they are, choose **Show Paragraph Marks** from the 'View' menu and all page breaks and new paragraphs will appear in the text allowing you to select and delete them.

Pictures

Adding a picture to your newsletter is easy. Simply choose **Picture** from the Insert menu, and then choose **From file**. A dialogue will appear allowing you to select your picture from anywhere on your hard disk. Pictures will be automatically re-sized to fit the column width, but you can drag on their corners to expand or shrink them.

Right click on a picture, and choose Format and you can add a border around the picture. Select the Layout tab and you can define the way text flows around your picture. Here are the options:

In line with text – places the picture in your document in just the same way as it would an extra large letter. If there's room on the line before or after the picture, the text will continue otherwise, the text will start again on the next line. This layout is useful if you want to use the picture to break up the text.

Square – places the picture in the middle of the text. You can drag it around anywhere on the page, and the text will arrange itself on either or both sides of the picture. This can be a great way to place an image in a large article without disturbing the flow of the text.

Tight – similar to Square but with less empty space around the picture. If your image has a transparent background, the text will flow right up to the edges of objects within the picture.

Behind text – the picture is placed behind the text and the text flows over it. Use this formatting only on very pale images you want to use as backgrounds. Think carefully about readability before you select this format.

In front of text – the picture is laid over the text, so unless it's transparent, you won't be able to see what's behind it.

TIP: TITLE

To create an image with a transparent background, you need to delete the background (even if it's plain white) in an image editor, then save it as a TGA, TIF, PNG or GIF file.

Adjustments

However you choose to place your picture, there are a few adjustments you can make to it within Word that will help with your layout:

Scale and rotate – click on any image in your document and you can move it around by dragging. You can scale it uniformly by dragging on a corner, and you can stretch it by dragging on one of the white dots at the centres of the edges. Above the image there's a green dot. Dragging on this will rotate your image.

Contrast and brightness – when you select a picture, a floating toolbox will appear. This allows you to do a little basic editing of your image. There are buttons for increasing and decreasing the contrast and brightness of the image (useful for making the picture clearer or for fading it out for use as a background image behind text).

Colour – there's also a colour tool for brightening colour or reducing your image to black and white. This is useful if you're going to be printing in black and white as it allows you to see the page as it will print. The Automatic and Washout options are also useful for strengthening or fading the colour in your shot.

Cropping – you don't always want to use the whole of your image, and the cropping option allows you to cut the image down to just the important details. You can cut an image down as much as you like, and make it any size or shape, but bear in mind, if you expand a small portion of a picture to fill a page, its quality when printed might not be very high.

TIP: MORE IMAGE OPTIONS

If you want more sophisticated control of your image you'll need to load the picture into a specialist image editing program. See the next chapter for details.

HINT: DON'T PANIC

Nothing you do to an image within Word has any effect whatsoever on the picture on your disk. You're only ever editing a copy, so don't worry about damaging your precious photos. You can't.

The most flexible method

The method used before is easy enough to master, but it's not very flexible. Your columns are as Word wants them to be and you can't be very creative in your layouts. In addition, it's hard to manage your publication so that everything fits perfectly into the spaces provided for it, and if you've got a long newsletter, laying it out can often feel like a cumbersome process.

However, there's another, more flexible method. It takes a bit of getting used to, but it's well worthwhile if you produce your newsletter regularly and want to give it its own unique look and style. This method has a lot more in common with professional publishing practices:

1 Create a blank document by selecting **New blank document** from the file menu. Start a new document and save it to disk. Use the zoom tool on your tool bar at the top of the screen to zoom out until you can see the whole page. In this method, we don't start with a body of text. Instead, we start with an empty page, and create boxes into which the text will be imported.

2 Create a box. Select **Text Box** from the Insert menu and choose **Horizontal** to create a box. A box is created for you, but ignore it and instead, click and drag from the top left to create a box right across the page about an inch deep. This will contain the title for our publication.

TIP: LEARN THE LINGO

If you're using Open Office, text boxes are called Frames.

3 Create another horizontal text box in the same way. This one will contain the headline, so make it a big, square-ish box just below the title box.

4 Now create four more boxes. This time, make them tall enough to reach to the foot of the page. These will contain the main text of your article.

5 Already, the page is beginning to take shape, and we haven't even added any text. We can see how the front of our newsletter is going to look. What's more, this layout is far easier to adapt than the previous one. Click on the edge of any box to change its size or shape or move it around. Make the headline box half the width of the page and move it to the left with two body text boxes underneath. Now stretch the second two body text boxes up to fill the gap on the right. Already you've created a layout you couldn't have produced using the previous method.

HINT: ADAPTING

The great thing about this is that you can constantly adapt the size and shape of any element on your screen without worrying about how it affects the rest of the pages. If your text is slightly to long or short to fit on the page, it's easy to adjust the size of the headline or pictures slightly to make everything fit perfectly.

6 Now it's time to add some text. Open another document containing some text. If you've got a sample article, use that, but any text will do. Now select the main body of the text and choose Cut from the Edit menu. Move back to the newsletter document, click in the box in which you want the main text to begin, and select **Paste** from the Edit menu.

7 Your text now appears in the box. Click on it, and choose **Select All** from the Edit menu (or press ctrl-A) and all the text is selected. Right click and choose **Font** to pick the typeface and size for your text as in the previous tutorial.

8 If there's more text than there is space in the box, it will simply disappear out of the bottom of the box. You need to tell any excess text where to go. This is easy, just right click on the edge of the box and choose **Create Text Box Link**. The cursor changes to a paint bucket. Now click the box representing the next column of text and the text in the second box will start from the last line of the previous box.

TIP: OPEN OFFICE

Open Office uses a slightly different technique. Double click on the edge of a box, choose the **Options** tab and you can select the name of the box to link to or from. Linked boxes are joined by a line (which is invisible on the printed page).

9 Do the same for the other two columns. Your text should now flow from one column to the next. You've now set up an article. The flexibility in this system is obvious. You can continue to re-shape, move, stretch or shrink the boxes to re-arrange your page, and the text will automatically adjust to flow from one box to the next.

10 You can now add a headline in the headline box, and type in your publication's title in the top box. You can change the font size to add sub-headings if you want to, just as before. You can even divide the boxes themselves into columns if you like. In fact anything you can do using the previous method in terms of formatting your page, you can do in this method within a box.

TIP: SELECTING ALL TEXT

Click in a box and choose **Select All** from the Edit menu and Word will select all the article text even if it's spread over several boxes.

---

11 To create another page, click at the bottom of the existing page (outside of any boxes) and choose Break and Page Break from the Insert menu. This creates a new page on which we can create a new layout. This time, we'll create a news page. We lay out several boxes of different sizes to fill the page. We want one main news item, so we link the first two boxes together. The other boxes we leave – they'll each contain a single news item, so we don't need to link them.

TIP: DUPLICATING BOXES

You can copy and paste boxes in the same way you do with words, so to keep box sizes uniform throughout the publication, just duplicate the boxes and move them to another page.

Adding pictures in this method

We can add pictures just as before – by selecting Picture from the Insert menu. This places a picture wherever the cursor is – resizing it automatically to fit the width of the text box it's in. However, you can't use the layout box to make the text flow around the picture inside a text box.

You can also create pictures in boxes. Create a new text box of the correct size, click in it and insert the picture there. That way there's nothing in the box except the picture, and you can arrange it on the page with the other boxes.

Note: When resizing a text box with a picture in, you have to resize the box and the picture separately. Click on the picture itself to resize the picture, then click on the edge of the box to re-size the box.

---

12 Borders and colours

By default, boxes are all surrounded by black lines. You probably won't want these lines around every box in your finished newsletter, but they're useful during the design process. To remove them, right-click on the box edge and select **Format Box**. The dialogue which appears allows you to customise your box, altering or removing the lines, and even changing the background colour.

---

13 Next issue

When designing your newsletter's layout, the aim is to create a format for the pages which can be used for every issue. If you save your pages laid out as empty boxes for feature articles, news items, etc. then all you'll need to do next issue is to take the appropriate articles and paste them into the right boxes. If you've written news items, features, etc. of similar lengths, you'll only have to do minimal adjustments to your design, change the pictures, and add headlines, and you're done.

TIP: CREATE AN EXTRA PAGE FOR 'JUNK'

As you work on an issue you'll sometimes want to add or delete boxes on a page. If you think you might need them later, just drag them to the junk page, and you can easily retrieve them if you need to.

Kerning

One final term you might have heard applied to the layout of pages is Kerning. This is basically fine tuning applied to the spacing between letters, particularly in headlines, to make them more visually appealing. It's possible to change the letter spacing of individual pairs of letters or whole sentences by selecting them and choosing the Character Spacing tab on the Font format menu. Professional typographers spend a lot of time and effort on kerning to produce the best possible look for their headlines. Most of the rest of us don't even notice, so unless you've got plenty of time, and a readership of pedants, it's probably not worth doing.

THE ARTY STUFF

By now, you should be able to create a layout for the pages in your newsletter, and have a pretty good idea of what is or isn't possible in Word. That's the technical side of your publication's formatting, but we haven't yet covered the creative rules about what makes words and pictures look good on the page.

That's the subject of the next chapter as we explore the creative aspects of page layout.

4 Page Layout

In the last chapter we looked at a few of the basic tools available to the Newsletter editor in Microsoft Word. Word is by no means the only tool for laying out your newsletter, but whichever package you're using, the same rules of design apply.

In this chapter we'll be taking a look at some of those rules and how the creative process for designing your magazine works. We'll be looking at different shapes, formats and looks, and discovering how to use photos and illustrations to create a unique but recognisable style for your magazine.

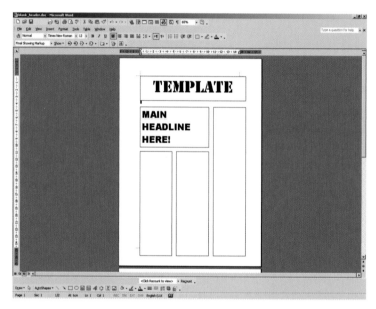

Creating a blank template for your newslatter is the best way to start

A NEWSLETTER WITH NOTHING IN IT

First time newsletter designers often make the mistake of trying to design their magazine 'live' at the same time as creating the first issue. In reality, it's far better to separate the design of the magazine itself from the design of each issue of it. If you start off by trying to construct the layout of the magazine around the articles and items you already have to put in the first issue, then you'll find that you need to re-design the magazine every time you produce a new issue.

If, on the other hand, you create a layout – a kind of blank template – and then cut and commission your articles to fit that template then you'll find that it's much easier to slot each issue together because you'll already have an idea of what goes where. Not only that, but you'll also find it easier to work out what you need to write to fill the magazine because you'll already know broadly what it's going to look like, how many feature articles you have, what length the news items will be, what information you need to get about upcoming events and what the front cover will look like. In other words, what you need to create before you start is an issue of the magazine with nothing in it.

SIZE AND SHAPE

Your first decision in laying out your magazine
is what its size and shape will be. Here are a
few options:

An A4 booklet suits a newsletter with a lot of content

A4 corner stapled Probably the easiest format
you can go for. The paper is a standard size
available anywhere. The printing is straightforward
(page 1 with page 2 printed on the back, etc.).
However, the results can look decidedly amateur.
This won't look like *Vogue*.

A4 leaflet A small newsletter can be published as
a single sheet leaflet folded twice in a 'Z' shape. This
is easy to produce, and cheap enough to use full
colour printing if you want to, but you won't be able
to get much in it, and if you need extra pages, you'll
have to switch format.

Thermal, or book-style, bindings can be pricey

A5 booklet A very popular format. Again made
from standard A4 paper, but here each sheet is
folded in half to produce 4 pages. The booklet is
held together with two staples in the centre. This can look very professional, but it's not too expensive.
In addition, you can print the front and back pages on a thicker paper (and possibly in colour) to create a
stylish magazine.

A4 booklet Exactly the same as an A5 booklet only it's printed using larger, A3 sheets. This can be more
expensive, but if you've got the budget (and a lot of content to fill it) the result is an impressive looking
publication which will fit in along side other newsstand magazines.

Other paper shapes You can have your magazine printed in any shape you like (many newsstand
magazines are slightly squarer than an a4 page), but doing so means printing on the nearest standard
sized paper and then cutting each page down to size. This takes time (for which your printer will charge)
and means using more paper.

Perfect binding (and other thermal bindings) This is the kind of binding used for books. Each sheet is
stuck to the spine of the magazine. You can have any even number of pages, but you really should have a
heavy cover and back page, and you need to be publishing a pretty substantial journal to justify the costs
of perfect binding.

TIP: FOLDING SHEETS AND IMPOSITION

If you're creating a newsletter from folded sheets of paper – i.e. anything that looks like a book – you'll need to give careful thought to the layout, or imposition, of the pages.

You'll be printing on paper twice the size of your magazine, and folding it so you have four pages on each sheet, and you can't just create pages 1,2,3,4,5 etc. in that order in your layout document.

Which pages will be placed where will depend on how many pages your publication has in total. For example, the first two pages will have to be printed on different sides of the same sheet of paper. However, the final two pages will also be printed on the same sheet with the last page printed next to the first. The only sheet containing four consecutive pages will be the centre spread where the magazine is stapled. If the magazine has lots of pages, there may be even more complex arrangements where different sections are folded together. All of which will make your head explode if you think about it too much. See the example below for a 16-page booklet. There are eight pages on the front of the sheet, and the corresponding eight pages on the back. After printing, the paper is folded in half vertically, so page two falls against page three, then it is folded again horizontally, so page four meets page five, and then it is folded yet again, so that page nine meets page eight.

Note: you might be able to simply supply each page to your printer as a separate file and let them handle which page goes where, but they will charge you for doing it.

The important thing to realise is that you have to know how many pages you're going to print and work out what that means for your page layout before you start. There's also another important consideration. If you're printing folded sheets, you're printing four pages at a time, so your magazine can only be 4,8,12,16, etc. pages in length if you want to avoid leaving blank pages. You can't create a 6-page publication using folded paper.

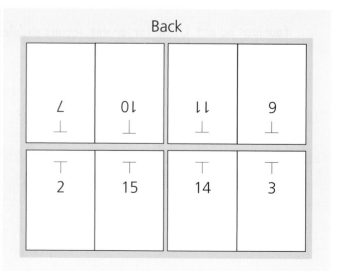

PAGE BREAKDOWN

The next step is to do a page breakdown for your magazine. Decide what will happen on each page, so that each page can be designed to fit the appropriate text and images. Remember, you're not designing a particular issue right now, just a typical one which contains all the elements that will regularly appear.

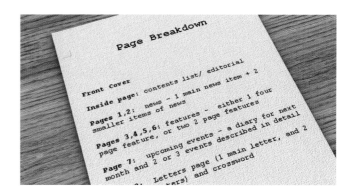

Example breakdown

• **Front cover**

• **Inside page:** contents list/editorial

• **Pages 1,2 NEWS** – 1 main news item plus 2 smaller items of news

• **Pages 3,4,5,6 FEATURES** – either 1 four page feature, or two 2 page features

• **Page 7 UPCOMING EVENTS** – a diary for next month and 2 or 3 events described in detail

• **Page 8 LETTERS PAGE** – 1 main letter, 2 smaller letters and a crossword

---

TIP: LOREM IPSUM

There's a problem all layout artists find when designing written documents. When you look at text on a page, you immediately and instinctively start to read it. So as soon as you paste in some text in order to try to work out how the page layout, fonts, etc. of your magazine look, you'll be constantly distracted by what the text says instead of how it looks.

The solution is to work with something you can't read, and the standard solution is to use a document written in latin:

'Lorem ipsum dolor sit amet, consectetur adipiscing elit. Praesent nisl dui, venenatis eget eleifend id, faucibus ac est. Ut ac tortor est, iaculis sodales metus. Praesent eget elit eget ante euismod imperdiet. Praesent tempus tincidunt lacus, et hendrerit eros adipiscing sed. Aliquam felis elit, molestie ut malesuada eu, dictum nec purus. Praesent nec nibh mauris, ac eleifend enim...,' and so on.

The standard page layout artist's text is from a piece of classical literature written in 45BC on the subject of ethics. It's used primarily because the length and arangement of words and paragraphs is pretty similar to modern English, but unless you read latin, it makes no sense, so your eyes will ignore it and concentrate on the way it's arranged on the page. You can download chunks of this text of any length you choose from www.lipsom.com ready to paste it into the text boxes of your own documents as you lay them out.

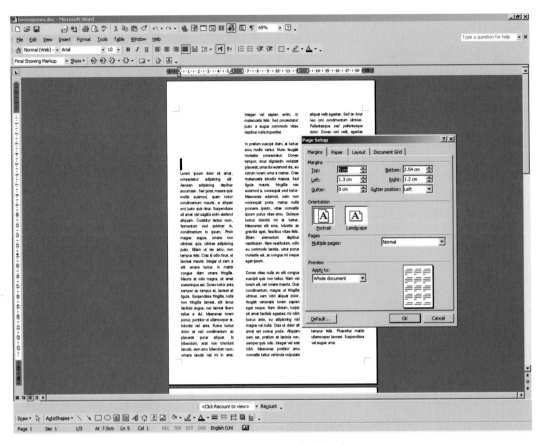

Laying out a page in Word

PAGE LAYOUT

You now need to work out just how much in the way of text and images you can fit on your pages. The first decision here is the number of columns you're using and the design and size of the font.

Start by opening your desktop publishing software and setting up the page size and shape (in Word, that's the page setup dialogue on the File menu). Now paste in your sample 'lorem ipsum' text and try out different sizes, styles and layouts (see chapter 3).

SELECTING ALL TEXT TO CHANGE A SETTING

To change a setting, simply use 'Select All' from the 'edit' menu (or click ctrl-A) and then alter your settings. If you're using text boxes for your layout, all the text in linked boxes will be selected. If you're not using boxes, all your text will be selected.

If your magazine is roughly A5 sized, a two column layout often works well, allowing you to comfortably fit in more text than a 1 column layout. If your journal is A4 sized try 3 or even 4 columns to a page.

TEXT ALIGNMENT

Most newsletters are left aligned rather than 'justified' – meaning that the spaces between the letters are always equal, but the ends of lines aren't aligned. This gives the reader's eye subconscious cues about where they are on the page, allowing them to locate what they're reading more quickly.

FONTS AND TYPE SIZES

Generally, you won't want to have the font for your main body text larger than roughly 14 point or smaller than about 9 point. This depends on the readability of the typeface you're using and how many words you want to get on a page. Text that's too small is unreadable and off-putting. Text that's too big suggests you've got nothing much to say, and are just filling space.

Some commonly used typefaces

Times New Roman Developed for the Times newspaper in 1931. This combines readability with authority. It's commonly used in all kinds of professionally produced documents and readers are used to seeing it in large blocks of text.

Arial Another very clear font. Less decorated than Times New Roman and with more empty space, it has a trendy, arty feel to it, so tends to get used in magazines which have less text and more pictures.

Courier New Like an old fashioned typewriter. Courier offers readability, but with a slightly less polished look. Choose it if you want your publication to appear more casual and hand-made.

Comic Sans Serif A font with a slightly hand-written look. It's still readable in blocks, but has a friendly, informal tone. Comic Sans Serif is often used by children's publications and clubs.

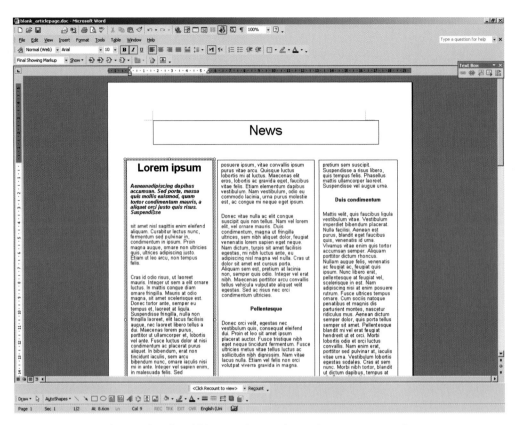

Heading styles should be consistent throughout your newsletter

HEADLINES AND SUB-HEADINGS

Headlines and sub-headings can be of the same font as your main text or a different font. However, most of the time fairly simple, bold fonts are used and they're often 'sans serif' fonts (typefaces without decorative embellishments).

They can be of any size, but you should have firm rules about what sizes and fonts you use where, so that each page and each issue of your magazine has a consistent look.

MINIMIZING YOUR USE OF DIFFERENT FONTS

As a rule of thumb, have just one font for headlines and one (different or the same) for body text. Use bold and italics within the text, but don't change font. Use unusual fonts only for main headings identifying your journal (i.e. the title, or section headings).

If one of your main article titles is 22-point Arial Bold, make sure they all are. If your sub-headings are 12-point bold, make sure they're all 12-point bold. This may seem pedantic, but it's not. Readers will subconsciously take in your decisions about fonts and use them to navigate through your publication.

When you pick up a familiar newspaper, your eyes scan straight to the items you want to read. You probably don't even notice that the sizes and styles of type are letting you know where one story and one section ends and another begins, and that the consistency of the layout means you always turn to the right page when looking for a favourite column, or the sports section. At least you don't notice until the publisher changes the layout, and you suddenly can't find anything.

WORD COUNT

Once you've selected the font and size and the number of columns, you'll be able to make a rough assessment of the number of words that will fit on a page of your magazine.

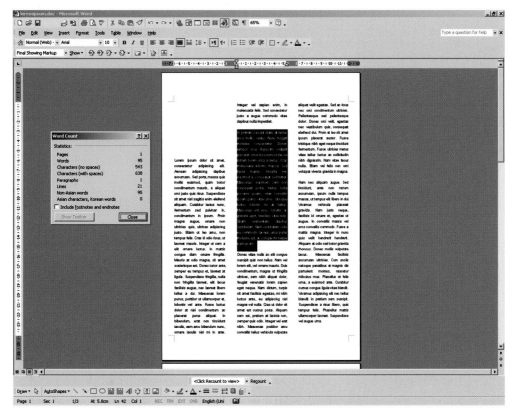

Checking word count for a section of a document

TIP: WORD COUNT

To find out the word count for your page using Word, select a page full of text (by clicking at the top and then shift-clicking at the bottom of the page) and then choose word count from the tools menu.

The word count per page in newsstand publications varies widely. A typical, roughly A4-sized magazine might have 600 words, a more pictorial magazine might have 200 words and a densely written journal might have 1500 words to a page. The word count will be an important factor in the layout you adopt.

ARTICLES

Your word-count will tell you how many words you need to write for your main articles, your news items and your other text, so make a list of the word-counts for each text item in your magazine. Once you know that you've got to produce 2 x 1200 word main features, 2 x 150 word and 1 x 300 word news items and so on every month, you'll have a much clearer idea of how your magazine will fit together.

What's more you'll be able to create a document to tell anyone writing for your magazine exactly what you require from them (see chapter 2).

From that point on, the whole process will run a lot more smoothly. Even if you decide to make exceptions every month, re-jigging to fit longer or shorter articles, it doesn't matter. The fact that you have a plan and you know how a typical issue fits together means that when you make a change – for example commissioning a 2000 word interview – you know exactly what that means in terms of dropping, shortening or lengthening other parts of the publication.

IMPROVING PICTURES

Pictures in magazines and newspapers are often a bit of a compromise. There's often one chance to get the shot you need, and if it comes out wrong, you've still got to use it. Just as often, there's no official picture at all, and you're forced to make use of a snapshot somebody happened to take on their mobile phone or point-and-shoot camera.

In cases like this you've got little choice, but there are a few things you can do to improve the look of your photos using a photo editing package. You'll need to do all your photo editing and save a finished version of your images before you bring them into Word (or whatever package you're using for your layout).

Here are a few easy things you can do to improve the quality of photos:

Auto Levels Most packages have an auto-levels feature which will search for the brightest and darkest pixels in an image, and use them to adjust the contrast and colours in the photo automatically. In other words, the contrast is adjusted so that the brightest spots in the image are white and the darkest are black. If you've got a washed out, over or under exposed image, this tool can make a massive difference.

Original, washed-out image   Image after using auto-levels tool

Red Eye If people in your photos appear to have red eyes, it's due to the flash from the camera reflecting off the interior of their eyes. Most photo editors have a tool allowing you to completely remove this effect.

Cropping Most photos need trimming at the edges – either to make them the right shape for the space you plan to put them in, or just to make them look better. Where you have people in shot, aim to trim it so they have 'Looking room' – i.e. if they're looking to the left, give them a little space in the photo to look into – don't just cut the picture off at the end of their nose.

Cropping a photo for better effect

Focus If a photo is blurry, there's very little you can do. Packages do offer 'sharpening' tools, but these just increase the contrast at the edges of objects. This can help if there's a little softness in the image, but they won't help improve a really blurred shot.

Grain Some programs allow you to remove the noisy dots produced when you photograph in low light, but bear in mind, these tools basically just blur the picture, so you'll have to sacrifice sharpness if you want to remove the grain.

Working on a grainy picture

Low resolution pictures If your photo has been taken at low resolution (i.e. on a phone) or compressed (i.e. it's come from a website), there may be fringing and blocky colours particularly in areas of subtle shading. Again, you'll have to live with this to some extent although adjusting the contrast and brightness may help to hide the effect.

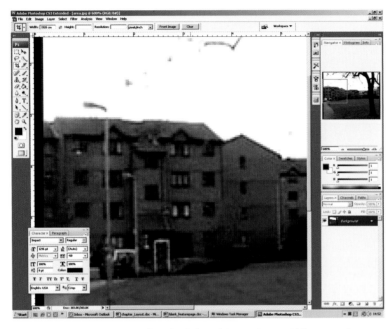

LOW RESOLUTION IMAGES
You can do a lot in image processing packages to bring out detail in images, but if it's not there in the first place, you can't create it. Likewise, just scaling up a photo in your image processing package doesn't get you any extra detail – a small image expanded will just become blurry.

You can't improve the level of detail in a picture if it's not there

TIP: WWW.LIPSOM.COM

There are a huge number of photo-editing packages on the market all with similar tools, but different approaches. Here are a few:

ADOBE PHOTOSHOP This is the industry standard used by most magazine publishers and everywhere still images are needed.

PHOTOSHOP ELEMENTS A cheap alternative for the amateur picture editor with a lot of the commonly used features of Photoshop, but an easier interface.

PAINT SHOP PRO Another reasonably priced package. It's not quite as easy to use as other offerings, but it has a wide range of professional tools.

MICROSOFT DIGITAL IMAGE SUITE A well organised package with easy to use one-click tools, but not a huge range of them.

THE GIMP A free alternative with a lot of features, but an intimidating interface with far too many buttons and menu items.

HEADERS

Your title logo needs special thought, and it's generally a good idea to use a distinctive (though readable) font. It's worth mocking up a few front covers with different looks and showing them to potential readers before you decide on a final image.

Remember, this is the one unique image which will allow readers to recognise your publication so it's important that it has impact and style and that it remains unchanged from issue to issue.

Title graphics are almost always placed full length across the top of the front page.

On the inside pages, you will probably want to divide the magazine into regular features. It's a good idea to design headers for these which can be used in every issue so that readers can easily navigate through the publication. These headers aren't quite as dramatic as the title graphic, but readers should be able to recognise them and differentiate them easily from the rest of the text.

THE FRONT PAGE

Front pages and covers are a law unto themselves. Most of the time they're re-designed for every issue and need similarities (so that the reader knows immediately that they're looking at your publication) but also differences (so they know there's something fresh and exciting that they didn't read about in the last issue).

The traditional point of a front page or a cover is to differentiate your publication from everything else on the newsstand, but even if you're not in that kind of competition, a strong front page is still important in getting readers to pick up your magazine and open it.

This is where newspapers and magazines differ:

Magazine covers give an overview of the content

Magazines

A magazine cover is designed to give the reader a taster of what's inside. Choose a couple of lines to describe the main features, and a big photo of something intriguing that the reader can learn about within.

Of course, you also need to provide the title of the publication in large, unique lettering, and it's customary to put the issue number, date, etc. underneath so readers know they're looking at the most up to date.

PUBLICATION DATES

In order to feel new and exciting, monthly magazines generally take their date as the month after they're published – April's issue goes out in March so it's read in April. This is pretty silly if you think about it because April's issue will have been put together in March, written in February and the ideas for its content may have been dreamed up and commissioned around Christmas. So in reality, if it's anything, it's the December issue.

Newspaper covers feature the most important story

Newspapers

Newspapers save their front page for their most important news item. It can be one story or several, but either way, use big, bold headlines and pictures to let the reader know at a glance the most important stories you're covering.

Be direct and to the point – if your readers don't know within a couple of seconds what the style, tone and main thrust of the issue they're holding is, then your front page has failed.

It's up to you how much or how little you put on the front page, but front page stories have to be of importance to everyone who receives the newsletter. They have to deliver significant information in an up front and clear way and they need to entice readers into turning the pages. Almost all stories that start on the front page end with a note along the lines of 'continued on page 5' or 'read the full story inside'.

Front page headline font sizes don't have to follow the rules set down in the rest of the publication. Generally, the more important the story, the bigger the headline and the shorter the words.

CONTENTS PAGE

If you're creating a magazine-style layout (rather than a newspaper style one), it's a good idea to have a contents page. List each of your main sections and features, and write a small (10–20 word) introduction to each section, giving the page number. You can add some small photos if you like, but keep the layout easy to read. Contents pages often make up half a page, with the editorial opposite.

NEWS PAGES

Traditionally, the first few pages of a newsletter are dedicated to hard news. This usually means several short articles – typically between 50 and 250 words long.

You never know what news you're going to get, but you can plan that you're going to have, for example, one main story, two smaller stories and three or four little news 'bites' in each issue. This calls for a flexible yet tight layout. Here are a few tips:

Develop a 'news sense' Try to get a very strong idea of what's most important to your readers and use that to rank your stories in order. Put stories higher up either if they're more immediate or if you have something in your article the readers won't have already heard somewhere else.

Build the page around your top story Then put the bigger stories at the top of the first page, working towards smaller, less important stories as you go down.

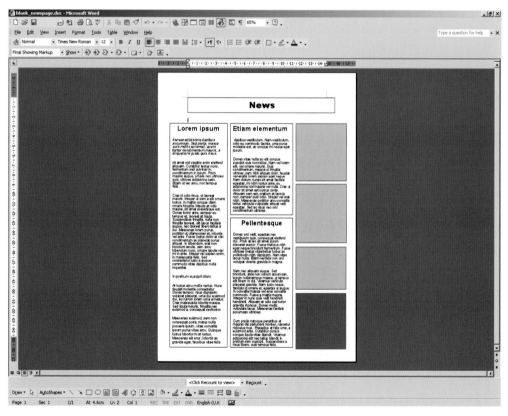

Designing a news page

Build around the pictures if your stories are driven by pictures If not, your headlines need to be powerful and instantly eye-catching.

Create a layout which leads the reader through the page News pages are necessarily more cluttered than the rest of the publication, so make sure it's very clear where one story ends and the next starts. Use simple lines, boxes, pictures and space to clarify where everything is for the reader.

Try putting stories of similar types together Perhaps you have news of several upcoming events – if so, put them all in a group on the page. Maybe you've got a couple of items of news about club members – if so, create a 'club news' sub-heading and give those stories a different coloured background.

Stick to your rules on type sizes and fonts With a lot going on on the page, the consistency of your type is even more important than ever.

Simplify The clearer the layout the better. You might have a lot of very different information to pack in, and have little choice about pictures, so keeping unnecessary decoration and clutter to a minimum is essential.

FEATURE PAGES

Feature articles tend to be longer, and more relaxed than news items. Readers will be settling down to them rather than glancing at them on-the-go so the layout should usually have a more laid back look.

Use a few well chosen pictures to decorate and illustrate the text. Choose the best looking picture (not necessarily the most informative one) to put at the top of the piece, and make it big. Features often start with a full or half page photo or illustration. Think of these big images as the punctuation that breaks up your layout – telling readers they're about to get something different in tone and content from what they saw on the previous page.

Headlines are less important in features. A good title is important, but you don't have to use huge print. Use small sub-headings to break up big blocks of text.

You can afford to use slightly larger type for features. There's not such a premium on densely packed information, so lay the page out for a relaxing read.

Place pictures wherever the amount of text looks too overwhelming – not necessarily right next to where the subject of the picture is discussed in the text.

Pull out quotes. Where you don't have a picture, take a brief quote from the article and arrange it in large type in its own box. You can even use a different colour. Use these quotes to tease the reader with interesting titbits about what's coming up in the text.

Leave space. In laying out features, you can afford to leave bigger gaps between columns and pictures, and within the text. You have much more opportunity to be creative with your layout than in more cluttered pages, and much more opportunity to give your publication a distinctive feel.

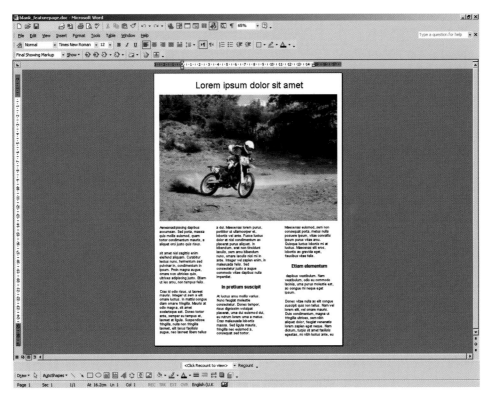

How a feature page may look

ADVERTISING

If your publication contains advertising, you can either place it throughout the magazine or in a given section (usually near the back).

Advertising throughout the magazine can make things untidy, but it can also help the layout – allowing you to fill gaps where articles are too short to fill a page. Most professional magazines keep advertising on a separate page from articles, but newspapers don't have such a division.

Advertising in its own section is easier to control and lay out. It's also easier to sell because you know you've got a given number of 1-page, 2-page, and 3-page slots to fill. If you have a gap, you can always use it to advertise your advertising team – 'phone this number to advertise here'.

THE BACK PAGE

Traditionally, the back page is where your publication becomes a little less formal. Letters, quizzes, crosswords, cartoons and other, more interactive chatty items appear. This is your newsletter's social page, so reflect that in your layout.

This page has to feel a bit different from the rest of the magazine, so you can afford to break a couple of your layout rules here. Have a bit of artwork or a different logo to introduce the page, use colour or shading to mark the page out.

Note: Don't forget, if you're using a folded format, and you're printing your front cover in colour, you'll also be able to put colour on your back page because it's on the same side of the same sheet of paper.

Try making readers' letters a little less formal – use a less austere font like comic sans serif or courier, and try placing each letter at a slightly different angle on the page.

Consider giving the page a themed look – like a notice-board with pieces of paper pinned to it, a web-page, or a club-house.

You don't have to stick to straight columns here if you don't want to. Think of the page as a collage and place the different elements however they look good. A little roughness in the arrangement helps to make the page approachable – but don't assume that means it's less work. Making something look artistically haphazard is harder than making it look neat.

Ignore these rules. It may be that the rest of your magazine layout has a relaxed, chaotic look. That's OK (if done carefully and deliberately). Equally, it may be that you want your back page to be as formal as the rest of your publication. That's fine too – the Financial times doesn't put it's readers' letters at a jaunty angle, and people still write in. As long as you consider what you're going to do and do it with care and consistency, it will work.

GOING LIVE

Once your magazine is designed and laid out, you're ready for the most thrilling, but also the most potentially costly part of your publication – printing it. In the next chapter we'll be looking at how to navigate the options and limitations of printing your publication, how to deal with professional printing firms, and how to solve potential problems before they happen.

5 Publishing

Once you've done all the research, written your newsletter and laid it out on the page, you'll need to move to actually getting it printed. This chapter will take you through some of the possibilities and pitfalls involved in giving your newsletter from the computer screen on to the printed page.

LAYOUT

In designing and laying out your newsletter you will already have some idea about how you want to get it printed. This might be a very simple format – A4 pages printed in black and white on standard paper and staples at the corner. On the other hand, it might involve colour printing, glossy pages, folded paper leaves, or even book-style binding.

PRINTING PROCESSES

There are several possible processes you can use to have your newsletter printed and the one you choose will depend on your budget, the number of copies you intend to print, and your colour requirements.

Home printing

If you only need to produce a few copies, you might consider printing your newsletter on your home printer. The advantage in doing this is that you have complete control over how it looks, you can use colour as much as you like, and you can choose the paper as well. In addition, you can print as many or as few copies as you like.

Home printing gives you colour flexibility

The disadvantage is that page for page, Home printing can be quite expensive (work out how many pages you get out of your print cartridge, how much it costs, and how much your paper costs, then add in the price of electricity, and the cost of replacing the printer itself when it wears out). Home printers tend to be slow, they don't respond well to dealing with hundreds of pages at a time, and they can't usually print right to the edges of the paper.

Single-colour printing

The cheapest way to print at a professional printers is to use black ink on white paper. You can use different colour inks or different colour papers for very little extra money, but black and white is usually more readable, and works better for illustrations and photos. With single colour printing you can produce lots of copies very quickly and cheaply, and the results will be crisp and sharp.

Two- or three-colour printing

If you have a little more money, you can add in extra colours. Typically, you have the main text in black, with occasional spot colours – for example, in your headlines or title logo.

Colours can be chosen from a Pantone chart

So-called 'spot colour' inks can also be a little more adventurous. As well as normal colours (chosen from a pantone chart), you can use metallic gold or silver inks, fluorescent or luminous inks, or even inks with unusual textures and finishes (for example glossy inks).

It's worth using these special effect inks with a little restraint. Tabloid newspapers often used to be printed in black and white, but with a single colour (usually red or blue) to highlight the titles. However, repeated use of spot colours throughout the newsletter can look distracting and unprofessional.

Four-colour process printing.

Four colour printing uses four inks: cyan, magenta, yellow and black. The document to be printed is separated into four elements, each containing a single colour, and the elements are printed over each other. By mixing these colours, any colour or shade can be created. Four colour separation printing is the way that most coloured publications you read are printed.

The results are very good. Colour photographs reproduce very well as do illustrations and plain text. However, this method is expensive, and for that reason many publications reserve four colour printing for the cover, and occasionally a centre page spread.

PAPER

You can have your newsletter printed on a range of different types of paper. Generally, paper of about the same standard you would buy for your home printer is fairly cheap. It'll work well for most types of printing, and your publication will look reasonably good.

Paying more generally gets you thicker paper. Paper quality is measured in grams per square metre – gsm – so the heavier paper is the more expensive it will feel.

Copier paper is around 80 GSM, whereas a birthday card is around 170 GSM. Additionally, you can select different colours and different finishes for your paper.

Most newsletters are printed on nothing more substantial than 80 GSM paper. Newspapers (where the number of copies is often huge, but the quality doesn't have to be that high) are frequently printed on a much thinner paper.

Paper samples

Usually, the higher your print run (the more copies you intend to print), the more choice you have about printing techniques and paper. If you're printing several hundred or several thousand copies, the cost per copy will drop substantially (often, it can be as cheap to print a thousand copies as it is to print a hundred).

If your print run is into the high hundreds, you may be able to go for a glossy paper. This gives your publication a much more professional look and feel, creating something a lot more like a magazine.

BINDING AND FOLDING

To finish off your newsletter (assuming it's more than one page), you'll need to consider how it's folded and bound. At the simplest level, this might mean a staple placed in the corner. A more sophisticated binding might mean the pages being trimmed to size, folded in the middle and stapled. You might consider adding a cover made from a thicker paper and printed in colour. If you have a much larger publication, running to 50 pages or more, a binding with a proper spine might be needed.

All of these things are possible, and can be done by your printer (at an additional cost). If your print run is big enough, your printer might even offer the service of posting out your magazine, but again, you'll have to pay. Alternatively, you can take home your printed pages, and assemble the publication yourself.

It's worth contacting a printer when you're deciding on the number of pages, size and circulation of your newsletter to find out what the options are, and how much they're likely to cost.

FORMATS

Once you've agreed with your printer on what the magazine will eventually look like, you'll need to deliver it to them. Here are a few things, they might want to discuss with you:

A 50dpi quality jpeg

Image resolution – a photo on a computer is made up of thousands of dots – each one of a different colour. The more dots, the higher the resolution of the photo and the clearer it will be when it's printed. Most printers would like to print photos at a resolution of 300 dots per inch (DPI). In other words, if you want your photo printed an inch across, it will need to be at least 300 dots across. If you want it to be printed 6 inches wide, it'll need to be 1800 dots across. You can stretch a 300 dot image right across the page if you want to but the bigger it is the more blurry it will look.

When laying out your page, get the highest quality pictures you can, look at their resolution, and bear the 300 DPI rule in mind. However, if you have a picture in lower quality, and you need it to be printed larger, then (whatever your printer tells you) it can be done – you just have to be prepared for the quality to be limited.

A 300dpi quality jpeg

Print mode – as we have already seen, full colour printing is done by mixing, cyan, magenta, yellow and black inks. This is known as CMYK colour. However, colours on a computer screen are created using red blue and green light. This is known as RGB colour. Now, to most of us, the difference between these two systems is pretty academic. Colour is colour. However, there are slight differences in tone and shade between equivalent CMYK and RGB colours, and it's a printers job to care about that.

Cyan, magenta, yellow and black inks

Your printer should be able to deal with any inconsistencies for you, but you should bear in mind that because they're created differently, the colour on your computer screen won't look exactly like the colour on your page. This becomes most obvious when you have similar colours or colours at a similar brightness next to each other on the page. It's possible for coloured text which is quite contrasting on screen to be unreadable once printed.

ON-SCREEN COLOUR

One additional problem with print and screen colours is that everybody's screen is slightly different just as every batch of ink and every paper is different. Your image editing package may let you set your screen up to certain standards, but the only way to check your colour is to see a printed proof.

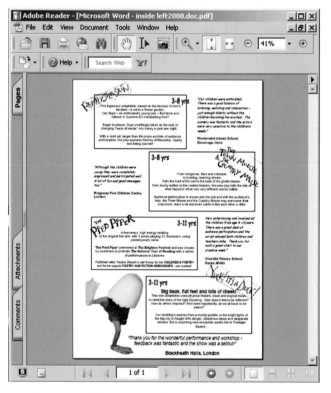

Creating a PDF of your file will protect the layout

Unfortunately you can't just deliver a file from your word processor (or whatever software you are using to lay out your newsletter) to your printer. There are two reasons for this. The first is simply that they may not be using the same software. The second is that the fonts installed on your computer might be different to those installed on theirs. If you've used anything other than Arial and Times New Roman, the chances are, another computer – even one running the same software might not have the same fonts.

If they don't, the computer will have to replace your font, with one it does have, and this will inevitably be a different style and a slightly different size, which in turn will throw your carefully constructed page layout into chaos.

And the fonts themselves are pieces of artwork which designers have created and licensed to software companies. In other words, although you're allowed to use them in your own documents, they are subject to copyright, and you can't just send them to your printer.

The solution is the PDF (Portable Document Format). PDFs basically wrap up everything in your document, including fonts, images and text, into a single sealed file. This allows the printer to print your document, but doesn't allow them to use the fonts in their own documents.

It's a convenient file format that anyone can open and it will reliably reproduce the same layout on any computer.

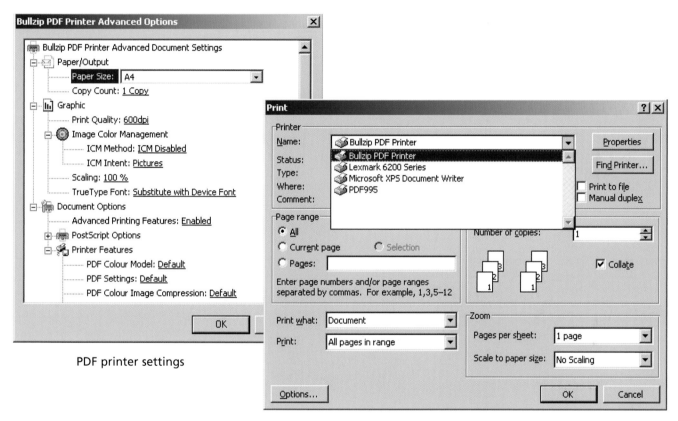

PDF printer settings

Printing a PDF

HOW TO PRODUCE A PDF

Word for Windows can't, on its own, create PDF files (although OpenOffice can simply by choosing 'Export as PDF' from the file menu).

Luckily, there are several free pieces of software, which will allow you to 'print' a document to a PDF file. Search online for 'pdf printers' (a good one is 'Bullzip pdf printer', but there are many others).

Once the package has been installed, it acts just like a printer in all your software packages. Simply choose 'print' from the file menu, and use the dropdown list on the printer dialogue in Word (or whatever package you're using) to select your PDF printer instead of your normal printer.

Now, instead of printing on your desktop printer, your document will be converted into a PDF file, and saved to disk. It's as simple as that.

The resulting file can be sent to your printer, and should contain everything they need to produce your finished newsletter.

CUSTOMIZING YOUR PDF

You may be able to customise your PDF printer through the Properties button in your print settings dialogue (depending on which pdf printer you're using). This allows you to customise the PDF produced, creating either a high quality, large PDF file (for sending to a professional printer) or a small, lower quality file (for putting on the Internet or emailing to subscribers).

FRONT AND BACK PAGES

The one thing the PDF file can't tell your printer is which files go on the front and back of each other. Typically, you'll produce a different PDF for each side of each sheet of paper that needs to be printed.

You'll have already thought this through when doing your layout (see chapter 4) but your printer won't know, so you'll have to name your files appropriately and explain to them exactly how it all fits together.

Here's an example: let's say you've got an A5 booklet style newsletter made up of a cover and 8 interior pages. This would be made up of 3 sheets of A4 folded in two, so you'd supply the printer with 6 PDF files which might be labelled:

- front_and_back_cover.pdf to be printed on the reverse of interior_front_and_back.pdf
- pages_1_8.pdf to be printed on the reverse of pages_2_7.pdf, and
- pages_3_6.pdf to be printed on the reverse of pages_4_5.pdf

Having the wrong pages printed back to back is one of the commonest and most expensive mistakes of the new newsletter editor.

TIP: SELECTING PAGES

If you've laid your magazine out as one document, you can select which pages get turned into a PDF by choosing them in the printer dialogue.

PROOFS

Always insist that your printer shows you a proof before going for a final print run. A proof is a single copy printed using all the same settings as the final prints. Check the proof carefully for errors in the layout, problems with colours, positioning on the page, paper quality, photo reproduction and overall look. If there's any problem at all with your newsletter, looking at the proof is your last chance to catch it.

Checking proofs

Choose recycled paper if you can

ENVIRONMENTAL CONCERNS

40% of the world's wood harvest is used for making paper, and the paper industry is the 4th largest creator of greenhouse gasses. Your printer should offer you the choice of using recycled paper for your printing. They should also be able to tell you the sources for the non-recycled paper – i.e. whether it's made from sustainable forests and what processes have been used in its production (look out for the use of chlorine to bleach the paper).

Paper is heavy and a lot of energy goes into transporting it, so it's also a good idea to take account of how far your paper has travelled to get to you, and try to focus on locally produced paper. Alternatively, see chapter 6 for a few options for 'digital publication' which are not only better for the environment, but also completely free for you!

DISTRIBUTION

Once your printer has completed the job, and supplied you with all the copies of your finished newsletter, you'll need to distribute it. After the excitement of picking up your beautifully bound, pristine copies this will seem like a bid of a drudge – and it's always a lot more work than new publishers imagine.

Here are a few quick tips for various distribution methods:

Posting copies to subscribers

If you're posting out copies, you'll need to develop a tight system for keeping tabs on names and addresses.

Keep a list in a form which you can easily update as new subscribers appear, or old ones drop off. It's a good idea to learn to use a database program which will keep track of your subscribers, but also allow you to print off address stickers so you don't have to write each envelope out yourself.

Budget for envelopes and stamps along with your printing costs – they quickly mount up. But also, factor in the volunteers you're sure to need to help you stuff envelopes. It's a thankless job, but as long as you keep your helpers in wine, pizza or cupcakes (depending on who they are), and make sure there are enough of them and the environment is social enough, you should get the job done with minimal fuss.

Postal distribution

Distribution through shops

If you're distributing to shops, or other venues, you'll need to keep account of who has how many copies and what's happening to them.

Make sure you plan for returns

You'll also need to be efficient in getting them delivered when you say you will, and in collecting money and unsold copies too.

Most shops will take copies on sale or return, so you should have a plan for what you're going to do with copies that come back at the end of the month (a good idea is to pick them up early and have a secondary – possibly free – way to distribute unsold copies).

Even if your newsletter is free, you'll need to keep a careful eye on where copies are going, and you'll need to adjust your print run and distribution for the next issue accordingly.

Door to door

Delivering your newsletter by hand street to street is a dull job, and if you don't have an army of eager minions to help, it can take up a huge amount of time. If you do have helpers, value them. They're as essential to your newsletter as the people that write it, and if they don't feel valued, you'll quickly loose them. As with all volunteers, keeping them fed is absolutely key.

If you're on your own, consider finding someone who's doing the rounds anyway (for example someone delivering take-away leaflets), and making them an offer for delivering your newsletter too.

Going online

By now, you should be able to take your written and laid out publication and get it produced. It's always great to see your finished work printed and bound and ready to thrust into the hands of subscribers.

However, nowadays, publication doesn't always mean producing a paper version of your work. Many magazines are partially delivered online and many more have gone completely digital, avoiding the expense and difficulty of real world printing entirely.

The next chapter will give you a few pointers about taking your publication into cyberspace.

6 New Media Publishing

Nowadays, most people have access to the Internet. Most people have email and most people have some idea how to use it. Broadband Internet is available almost universally, so sending complex documents with photos and even moving images is increasingly possible.

All of this opens up a whole new horizon for anyone creating newsletters. If you can distribute your publication (or at least some copies of it) digitally instead of on paper, you'll not only save money and time, you'll reduce your newsletter's environmental impact too. You can increase your readership to the thousands, or even hundreds of thousands without changing your production budget, and your subscribers can live anywhere in the world. You can even send copies to people while they're travelling.

There's also another advantage. An online newsletter – whether it's based on the web, or sent as an email can much more easily develop a relationship with its readers. If the reader of a paper magazine wants to contact the editor, they have to find their contact details, write a letter and post or email it.

However, if the same newsletter arrives by email, the reader is already sitting at their PC when they get it. if they read something they want to respond to, all they have to do is hit 'reply'.

Many people now read news online

WHAT'S HAPPENED TO THE PROFESSIONAL MEDIA?

The digital revolution is sweeping through the magazine and newspaper industry, and huge changes are taking place. As a newsletter editor, it's worth taking a bit of notice of how the big-boys have responded to the Internet, and learning their lessons.

Over the past few years, more and more people have started getting their news Online because websites can be far more up to date than newspapers, and so sales and advertising rates for newspapers and magazines have plummeted. Canny publishers have built up their websites, publishing important news Online as it comes in, and moving their print editions more towards analysis and investigative work rather than hard news.

Magazine websites often now include at least a taster of the content that can be found in the paper versions, and advertising is sold on the website as well as in the printed edition. Some magazines (particularly computer titles) make almost everything they publish in print available on their websites, and many titles produce articles specifically for the Internet version that never get into print.

Successful publishers also recognise that interactivity is one strength of the Internet. By encouraging readers to provide their email addresses, they build up mailing lists and send out regular mini-publications containing a few lines about interesting features or news items newly posted on the website.

Some smaller publications have even replaced their printed issues with newsletters sent by email.

But where does the cash come from in the new Online publishing industry? Well, the answer to that unfortunately is nobody's quite figured it out yet. Of course, you can put an advert in an email newsletter in just the same way you'd put one in a paper newsletter. Advertising on a website is also possible – web advertising does generate some money, and the good news is that it's easy to set up even if you're just a small website.

You can sell your adverts on a website directly in the same way you sell print ads, and get someone who knows how to edit your website to put them up. Usually, this involves creating a link to the advertiser's website from your own.

HOW TO SIGN UP FOR GOOGLE ADVERTISING

If this seems like too difficult, you can get someone like Google to do it for you. If you have enough visitors to your website, you can sign up to Google for free and allow them to place ads on your site. You'll get paid for the number of people who click on the ad.

1 Create a Google account (click at the top right corner of the www.google.com homepage) and set up an account.

2 Sign into your account and find the Google AdSense™ link. This will allow you to find out the details of Google's advertising offers.

3 Fill in the details of your website and apply to Google. They will respond by surveying your website, and if they accept it, sending you a piece of code to paste into your webpage. This code will automatically run adverts on your site.

Using Google Adsense™ can earn you money

4 Every time a visitor clicks on one of the adverts, you'll get paid a few pence.

The problem with this type of advertising is that you need a lot of visitors, or at least a very specific very focussed group of visitors to make anything more than pennies.

CHARGING

Aside from this, some newspaper publishers are experimenting with charging for subscriptions to their websites. This works particularly well for specialist titles with information you can't get anywhere else – scientific publishers for example, and financial newspapers . However, this is unlikely to work in the long term and Online publishers will have to find other ways to make money.

EMAILING YOUR NEWSLETTER

The simplest way to distribute your newsletter online is to simply send it out as an email. However, there are a number of ways to do this:

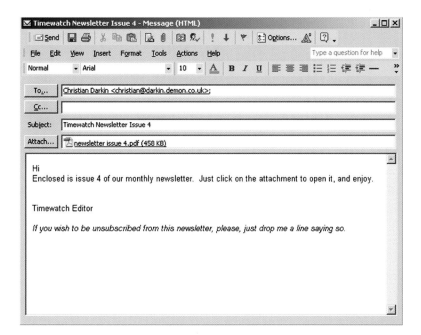

A PDF attachment

Perhaps the easiest method is to simply Create a PDF file of your publication (see chapter 5) and attach it to an email. Almost everyone with a computer will be able to open and read a PDF file, and it will come up identically on every computer no matter what its hardware, software and fonts.

To do this, just create an email in the normal way with a brief covering note, then click the attach button (the paperclip icon in Microsoft Outlook). This will bring up a dialogue from which you can locate your PDF on disk. The file will be loaded into your email, and sent with it.

SUBJECT HEADINGS

Give the email an appropriate subject heading (i.e. Parish newsletter June). Always make sure your subject heading follows the same format so your subscribers learn to recognise it and don't accidentally delete it as spam.

There are a couple of things to remember when sending PDFs:

Keep it small Most people have broadband, so they can tolerate large-ish files. However, avoid sending anything by email that's larger than about 2mb in size unless you know your recipients can receive it (to check the size of your pdf file, right-click on it in a folder in windows and choose the Properties option).

The chances are if you've produced your PDF for printing, it will be very large. This is mainly because your printers will want the highest possible quality photographs. However, for viewing on a computer screen, or even home printing, your readers don't need this level of detail. Look in your pdf printer settings and click the Advanced button to reduce the quality and therefore the size of your pdfs.

TIP: FILE SIZE AND QUALITY

The size of a pdf is usually defined by the resolution (for print it should be at least 300dpi, but for email, go for 72dpi) and the size of the document (A4, A5, etc.) as well as how many pages it has. Try different settings to work out the best balance of quality and file size.

Put the pages in order The PDFs you send to the printers will have their pages arranged so that the document flows correctly when folded and stapled. The back cover and front cover will be on the same printed sheet, and page numbers will be arranged for printing. In addition you'll probably create separate PDFs for each printed sheet.

This will make no sense when viewed on a computer screen. For online distribution, you need to arrange your pages in a logical order. Put all the pages into the same document (you should be able to simply select everything on the page, then use the cut and paste options from the Edit menu to move it into a new document), and put them in order starting with the front cover and ending with the back cover.

Consider hosting instead of sending Sending the PDF as an attachment means it's sent in its entirety to all your recipients. If you've got a particularly large newsletter or if you think not all your mailing list members will want to read the whole newsletter, try putting your PDF files up on a web page instead, and then sending out an email with a few lines about the contents of the issue, and a link to the web page. That way, people can choose to download it or not as they wish, and nobody gets sent a large file if they don't want it.

ARCHIVING PREVIOUS ISSUES

Having the issue uploaded to a website has another advantage. You can leave the link up permanently, so readers can, if they wish, look up previous issues just as easily as the current one. Your newsletter is automatically archived for as long as you keep the website going.

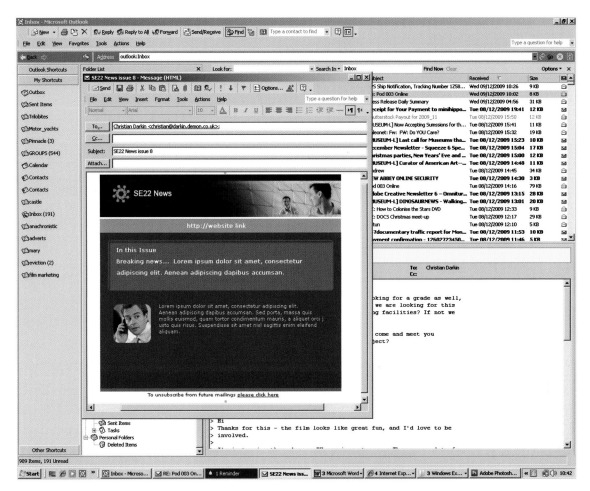

An HTML email is small but looks professional

An HTML email

You can send emails in the same html format as you create web pages. What this means in practice is that you can create a newsletter within an email in which only the text is sent to the reader, but any pictures are stored on your website. When the recipient opens the message, all the pictures are automatically downloaded as they're reading.

This has the advantage that the initial email is very small, but when it's opened, the pictures will appear just as they would if you visited the website. In addition, you can add links to more articles stored on web pages, further information on other websites, or even advertisers' sites if you want to.

The disadvantage is that if there's a problem with the website, or the Internet connection, the images won't appear, and the newsletter will look a complete mess.

Using tasters Many professional newsletters are sent out in this form, however and typically, they're arranged so that the initial email contains a list of stories and features and a couple of pictures. Each story has a taster (say 20–50 words) and a link to the website where the full article is waiting to be read.

The articles can remain online for reference long after the initial publication date, and crucially, because they're held on your website rather than in the email itself, you can continue to update the articles as news stories develop and more information comes in. Also, if you know how to do it, you can allow readers to add their comments to the stories, creating a discussion on the subject among your subscribers.

The main downside of all this is that your website needs to be pretty sophisticated to run this kind of content, and it needs to be constructed in such a way as to allow you to update it regularly. Also, you need to be able to write your newsletter in such a way that the images will be found and test it on several different computers before you send it out 'live'.

Getting expert help If you plan to do this, the best advice is to enlist the help of a friendly web expert who can set up templates for both the newsletter email and the website 'landing pages' on which the articles are posted. That way all you'll have to do is write your articles into the templates and make sure everything's uploaded and checked.

CASCADING STYLE SHEETS

The technical term for these templates are Cascading Style Sheets (usually known as CSS) – so that's what you need to ask your web designer for! Once they're set up, you visit the website, type in your password and then add the text and pictures to create new pages on your site.

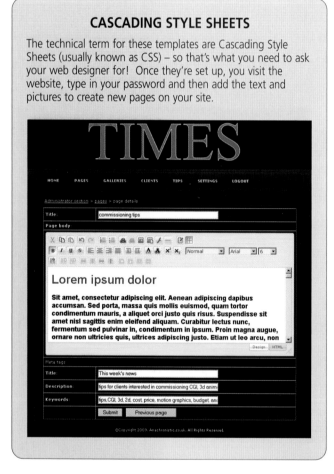

UNSOLICITED EMAILS

As a guide, if someone gives you their email address and tells you that they want to receive emails from you, then you're allowed to send them. However, you have to provide an easy way for people to let you know if they want to be taken off your mailing list (this usually means including instructions at the bottom of every email you send them) and you have to respond promptly when they do. If you're sending emails unsolicited, then you're on shakier ground, and you should look into the law in your own country.

Bulk emails

However you put your newsletter online, you'll need to notify your readers, and that means keeping and running a mailing list. People change their email addresses often and you need to make sure you add new subscribers and remove old ones efficiently.

This is all the more important because there are legal issues involved. Depending on the country you're operating from, there will be different rules on what information you can keep about people and what you're allowed to send them in terms of unsolicited emails.

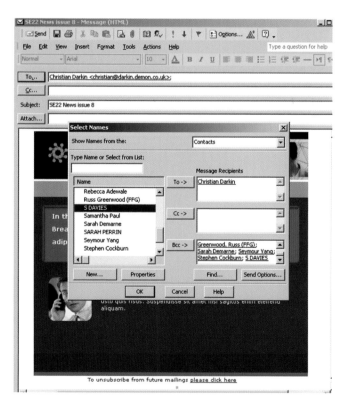

Sending bulk emails

How to email lots of people If you want to send emails to a lot of people at once, you could simply send lots of emails, but that's a bit of a pain. You can send a single email to a collection of people just by choosing their names in the 'to' section of your email program. However this reveals everyone's email to everyone else, so it's not a good plan.

A better method is to do one of the following:

Put your own email in the 'to' field, then put everyone else's email in the BCC field (in Microsoft Outlook, click the 'to' button to reveal the BCC field). This emails everyone on the list, but each person sees the email as being from just you to just them, so they don't know who the other subscribers are and when they hit 'reply all' they don't accidentally reply to everyone on the list.

Create a group (in Outlook click the 'to' button, then select New and choose new distribution list from the dialogue which appears). Name your group something like 'newsletter subscribers'). Now fill in all the email addresses to create your group. You can now select the group name and place it in the BCC field. The advantage of this method is that the group will be stored, so next time you want to email everyone, you don't need to re-enter all the addresses – just pick the group, and you're ready to go.

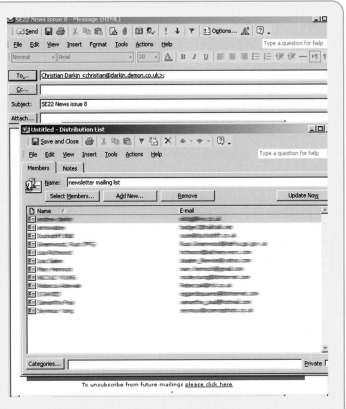

Setting up a bulk email mailing list

WRITING FOR ONLINE READERS

All the rules about writing for newsletters apply doubly for email and web news. The increasing popularity of hand-held devices such as the iPad may change the way people view the internet, but regardless of the technology, most readers scan it, instantly ignoring anything that doesn't grab their attention within a couple of seconds.

This means you need to be clear and succinct with your writing, and you need to make sure that the briefest glance at a headline or a photo will tell readers exactly what to expect from reading the full article.

Five words is a long headline on the Internet. 50 words is a long introduction. You should produce a contents page on which you aim to create a headline and introduction to every feature which will convince readers to click on the link to the main article within 20–30 words.

Once they do, pictures and good layout are key, and keeping readers' attention is difficult. Most written articles online are less than 500 words. If your feature is more than about 800, then it's likely that most readers will not get to the end of it – or if they do, will do so by skipping large chunks.

Economy of writing and an entertaining and engaging style are essential, and if you have more information than can fit into a 500 word article, try splitting it up. Provide links within the text to pages which explore certain aspects of your story more deeply. If that doesn't make sense for your subject, divide the article into several pages, each with a different heading (in the same way as you'd have sub-headings and boxouts in a printed article, make each of your sub-headings a new page on your site).

VIDEO

Online, it's as now as easy to add a video clip to your article as it is to add a photo. Video is becoming more and more accessible, and easier to use all the time. Mobile phones, webcams and stills cameras can be used to create video clips and your computer will already have a basic video editing package installed (look for Windows Movie Maker).

Video is becoming easier to use

If you learn to make use of this media and upload your video creations to a site like www.youtube.com (it takes about 10 minutes to work out how to upload video once you visit the site), then you can cut and paste a link directly into any web article you write.

In other words, if you're writing about an event and have a video clip from that event, you can upload it to youtube, and then paste the link into your article, so that visitors can watch the video as they read your write-up.

DISCUSSION

One thing the Internet is very good at is creating discussion. Visitors can, if you set up your website to allow it, post comments, and have discussions with each other. This kind of interactivity can turn your newsletter into a community, start friendships and connect you with your readers in ways a traditional newsletter could never hope to.

You can create forums on given subjects, or you can simply add comments boxes to the bottom of every article you post. If your site has been put together to allow it, you can restrict comments to members who have registered with you, or vet each comment before it's posted. On the other hand, you can allow unfettered access and let anyone post any comments they like. It's your decision.

> **TIP: DEALING WITH CONTENTIOUS POSTINGS**
>
> Occasionally, when a subject is very controversial, tempers can run high on Internet forums. You'll have to decide ahead of time what if anything you're going to do about arguments which get out of hand, and how you're going to respond when posters write to you asking for other posters' comments to be removed, or when insulting or even slanderous comments appear on your site.

READY-MADE SITES

If you want to get your newsletter online, but you don't have the patience or resources to create your own website, there is an easy answer – you can sign up with a site which allows you to post your articles and photos in a format you design with the features you want.

These fall into two categories; social networking sites like www.facebook.com and www.myspace.com and blogging pages. Both allow you to create an online presence, produce pages customised to your own look, and add to your site with pictures, text, videos and discussion forums.

The advantage of such ready made sites is that you can be up and running very quickly and they've already done all the technical design work for you. They're free, and they make adding extra elements like forums and video incredibly easy. They're very good at connecting you with other like-minded people all over the world, and creating a sense of community.

The downside is that there's a limit to the amount of customisation you can do to your page, and you generally can't sell advertising. The site concerned will also have some degree of control over your page and how it is viewed and may choose to change things at any time. In addition, as with anything that happens online, nobody will know what you've created unless you tell them, and a strategy for publicising your publication is essential.

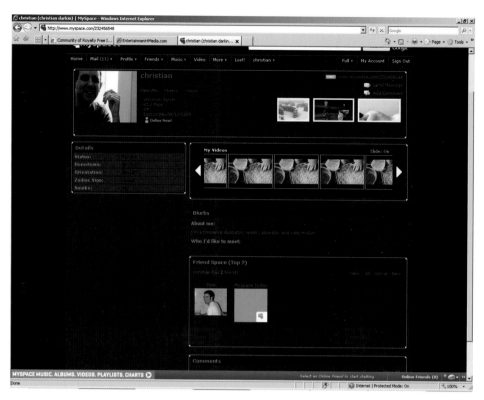

Social networking sites and blogs are a good way to reach lots of people

Social networking sites

Social networking sites basically allow you to create a profile. Most people create a profile for themselves, and use the site to talk to their friends. However, it's just as easy to set up a profile for a society or an organisation (although some sites are a bit iffy about commercial organisations creating profiles).

Your profile page can contain whatever you like, so adding photos, logos and news pages is pretty easy. If you have an event coming up you can publicise it, and if you have articles written you can include them on separate pages. Profiles can be updated as often as you like, and if you have other content on other sites, you can create links to that as well.

Anyone who's interested in your page can become your 'friend' (the equivalent of subscribing to your newsletter) and every time you update your site, all your friends will be notified and can come and take a look.

It's not a newsletter in the traditional sense, but it fulfils all the same functions, and has the added bonus of being both immediate and sociable.

If your page is well received, people will recommend it to their 'friends' and your readership will grow. Likewise, you'll quickly hook up with other people publishing pages on similar subjects and be able to swap information and ideas.

Blogging

A blog is basically an online diary and as such, it's a lot more like a traditional newsletter than a social networking page.

You can sign up to create a blog in about 5 minutes at sites like www.blogger.com and you can publish new entries on it as often or as rarely as you like. Each time you do, a new page is created including your text, pictures, videos and anything else you choose to add. You can even add a blog entry by simply emailing your text, so you can update your 'newsletter' very quickly and easily.

All entries in your blog are automatically archived, so anyone can search to find out what you said last week or last year. Likewise, most blogs have comments sections, so readers can add their own response to whatever you or other readers have said.

Blogs get archived by search engines (like Google) so new readers can turn up at your blog at any time just because you happen to be writing about something they're searching for information on. If they like what they read, they can subscribe to your blog and they'll be automatically notified whenever you post.

Blogs usually aren't as formal as a traditional newsletter, and they don't have recognised publication dates. They're often quite personal, but they don't have to be, and they're very easy to create and run. Well respected bloggers who know their subject and post often and interestingly on it can become quite well known in their fields and are often invited to comment in the mainstream media when news in their subject area breaks.

Whether your subject is cookery or politics, blogging is a great way to get your message across.

THE IPHONE REVOLUTION

Over the last couple of years, Internet surfing mobile phones like Apple's Iphone have really taken off. They provide a screen a few inches in size on which most Internet sites can be displayed, and most email formats received.

3G phones have made access to the internet much easier

These provide a way for users to read your newsletter wherever they are, and allow you to browse most websites, and even open PDF documents. However, because the devices are so small, most people's tolerance for reading long articles on them is even more limited than it is on a computer screen.

If you think a lot of your subscribers will be reading on their phones, here are a few tips:

1 Condense your text into just a few salient words on each story

2 Provide a link to longer articles for those who wish to read them

3 Concentrate on navigation – providing large, easy to find buttons for accessing different parts of your newsletter

4 Decide which links you think people will be looking for most often and make them large and obvious

5 Reduce all your buttons and menus to just a few important ones and keep them accessible

6 Don't use Flash. Flash is a tool website designers sometimes use to create animations and games. However, most phones simply won't display anything done in Flash.

HAND-HELD DEVICES

Devices like Amazon's Kindle, and the iPad are gaining in popularity, and for the first time, they offer a real alternative to the printed word in terms of portability and ease of use. In the long term such devices might become the standard format for most publishing. However, it's important to note that whatever the technology of the future, the basic ground rules for your newsletters will remain the same. Interesting content and strong layouts are going to be required no matter what the format of your work ends up in.

ONLINE PUBLISHING

It's up to you to what degree you embrace the online revolution. However, it does offer numerous cheap and easy ways to keep in touch with your readership. There's definitely still a place for the printed page, and there's still nothing to really replace the feel of a traditionally published journal.

However, it's a rare magazine that doesn't have some kind of online presence – whether that's a fully fledged website, a couple of pages on a social networking site or just an email contact for the editor, and digital publishing is definitely an avenue well worth considering.

FINALLY

In this book we've covered a huge range of skills and ideas. We've covered news journalism, feature writing, photography, design and layout. We've discussed content and style and explored the idiosyncrasies of different printing processes. We've looked at online publishing, stock photography and advertising.

Now, it's up to you to put all those skills into action. There's so much more to creating a newsletter than we've had room to explore here, but much of it you'll only learn by going out there and doing it. We hope this book will have given you the basic tools to get you started – and that once you have started, you'll start to relish the excitement of journalism, the artistry of design and the sheer panic of publishing deadlines that will drive you from issue to issue.

INDEX

NEW HOLLAND

First published in 2011 by New Holland Publishers (UK) Ltd
London · Cape Town · Sydney · Auckland

Garfield House
86–88 Edgware Road
London, W2 2EA
United Kingdom
www.newhollandpublishers.com

80 McKenzie Street
Cape Town 8001
South Africa

Unit 1, 66 Gibbes Street
Chatswood, NSW 2067
Australia

218 Lake Road
Northcote, Auckland
New Zealand

2 4 6 8 10 9 7 5 3 1
ISBN 978 1 84773 707 6

Senior Editor: Lisa John
Design: AG&G Books
Production: Sarah Kulasek
Publisher: Clare Sayer
DTP: Pete Gwyer

Reproduction by Pica Digital PTE Ltd, Singapore
Printed and bound by Times Offset (M) Sdn Bhd in Malaysia

Picture credits

All photographs © Christian Darkin, except for the following pages © Dreamstime.com: 7 /Monkey Business
Images; 8 /Stocksnapper; 9 /Drx; 13 /Trert; 14 /Diego Vito Cervo; 15 /Shevelartur; 19 / Julija Sapic; 20 /Glanum;
22 top/Vgstudio, bottom/Tomislav Birtic; 23 /Matt Antonino; 43 top/Celso Pupo rodrigues, bottom/Yury Shirokov;
59 /Chris Curtis; 60 /Joingate; 61/ Ana Vasileva; 62 /Izaokas Sapiro; 64 /Ron Sumners; 65 /Willyvend ; 65/ Becky
Swora; 66 /Peterfactors; 67 /Tyler Olson.

Google, Google AdSense and the Google logo are registered trademarks of Google Inc.